CAMBRIAN RAILWAYS

1859-1947

CYFLWYNIAD

I wyr Rheilffordd y Cambrian a fu'n fodd i greu
atgofion am wyliau hapus i filoedd a oeddynt yn
blant yr adeg honno; ac i'r bobol garedig hynny a'm
croesawodd ar eu haelwydydd ac a roes imi fenthyg
darliniau ac adrodd wrythyf bopeth a allent gofio
am yr hen Cambrian.

DEDICATION

To the men who made the Cambrian Railways work
and who made possible the happy hoilday memories of thousands who were children then; and to
the kindly people who made me welcome at their
firesides, lent me their pictures, and told me all they
could about the old Cambrian.

CAMBRIAN RAILWAYS

RAILWAYS

1859-1947

C. C. GREEN MBE

IAN ALLAN

Contents

Front cover: The lunch time train from Aberystwyth to Whitchurch was one of the Cambrian's traditional workings. Since the 1860s the time of departure had swung only a few minutes either way from 1 o'clock and it was at one time known as the 'South Express' because it conveyed through coaches for Birmingham and Paddington which were detached at Welshpool .Through coaches for the Manchester area went some three-quarters of an hour earlier via the 'North Express'.

The Great Western kept up the established order and here we see 'Earl' class No 3203 with Cambrian Jones Goods No 15 as 844 taking the 11 coaches of the 1pm ex-Aberystwyth up the Talerddig bank. Painted from a marvellous shot taken by Ifor Higgon on Bank Hoilday Saturday 6 August 1938.
Painting by George F. Heiron

Back cover: One of a batch of four 4-4-0 type express engines built by Sharp Stewart in 1895. No 84 was renumbered No 1107 by the GWR when the Cambrian was absorbed in 1922. A sister engine No 82 was smashed in the tragic head on collision at Abermule on 26 January 1921.
Painting by George F. Heiron

First published 1977 (volume 1), 1981 (volume 2)
Combined Edition first published 1997

ISBN 0 7110 2508 8

Published by Ian Allan Publishing

an imprint of Ian Allan Ltd, Terminal House, Station Approach, Shepperton, Surrey TW17 8AS.
Printed by Ian Allan Printing Ltd, Coombelands House, Addlestone, Surrey KT15 1HY

Code: 9703/A2

Bibliography

Books
Bowen, E. G. ; *Wales.*
Boyd, J. I. C.; *Narrow Gauge Railways in Mid Wales.*
Casserley, H. C.; *Preserved Locomotives.*
Christiansen & Miller; *The Cambrian Railways* Vols I & II.
Cooke, C. J.; *Swindon Steam 1921-1951.*
Cozens Lewis; *Books about the Cambrian Branches.*
Gasquoine, C. P.; *The Story of the Cambrian.*
Historical Model Railway Society, *Great Western Way* by J. N. Slinn.
Jones, Elvyn V.; *Mishaps on the Cambrian.*
Kidner, R. W.; *The Cambrian Railways.*
Mountford, E. R. ; *A Register of GWR Absorbed Coaching Stock.*
Railway Correspondance & Travel Society; *The Locomotives of the Great Western Railway* Vols 1 to 12.
Sir Felix Pole; *Pole's Book.*
Williams, David; *A History of Modern Wales.*
Wilson, R. B.; *Go Great Western.*

Periodicals
The Border Counties Advertiser.
The Cambrian News.
Great Western Magazine.
The Locomotive Magazine.
The Railway Magazine.

Recent publications
Green, C. C. , MBE; *The Cambrian Lines* Series:
    Coast, Vol I Machynlleth to Aberystwyth.
    Coast, Vol II Dovey Junction to Dolgelley

Author's Note

These were the first albums to have been designed around fully-informative captions. The second part especially gives a full account of how the Great Western dealt with the absorption of a Welsh Railway.

Of much interest were the many old locomotives and rolling stock given new leases of life. Thousands of locomotive photographs were taken by the Stephenson and other societies; but mostly in the yards when they were not in steam and not on running trains.

The accident picture at the top of page 152 originally suggested as happening at Llwyngwril is now known to have occured at Aberdovey.

Acknowledgements

J. Allman; G. E. Barratt; J. E. Benbow; D. Benjamin; R. Bennett; Birmingham Central Library; J. I. C. Boyd; H. W. Burman; John Burman; W. A. Camwell; R. S. Carpenter; K. Catchpole; G. H. W. Clifford; C. R. Clinker; Lord Davies; D. H. Davies; J. E. Davies; J. Elwyn Davies; J. S. Davies; W. J. K. Davies; George Dow; Dyfed (Aberystwyth) County Library; W. H. A. Edwards; R. J. Essery; F. W. Evans; J. A. Evans; W. Evans; T. H. Fenn; A. E. S. Fluck; W. R. Fryer; P. J. Garland; L. T. George; J. G. Griffiths, MA; A. M. Gunn; Lewis Hamer; F. W. Hannan; H. Harris; W. E. Hayward; F. E. Hemming; H. P. Higgins; Dr J. R. Hollick; Evan Howells; H. C. Hughes; J. Hughes; S. Humphries; W. Humphries; Hunslet Engine Co; Elfyn Jenkins; Isaac & Arthur Jenkins; Owen Jenkins; Ben Jones; B. T. Jones; D. Jones; E. C. Jones; Elwyn V. Jones; J. Jordan; John Lewis; J. M. Lloyd; O. Lloyd; Lord Londonderry; N. R. Miller; R. W. Miller; Dick Mills; H. Morgan; J. H. Moss; Colin E. Mountford; E. R. Mountford; The North British Locomotive Co Ltd; Miss A. Owen; David Owen; Mrs E. Owen; E. W. Owen; G. Owen; J. W. Owen; Mrs Nansi Owen; G. Archer Parfitt; R. Y. Pickering & Co Ltd; P. H. Pike; G. H. Platt; Albert Potts; Lord Powis; Powys Area Library; The Powysland Museum; John Rees; Harry Rees; J. P. Richards; F. S. Roberts; John D. Rogers; Ralph T. Russell; Salop County Library; T. Shuttleworth; J. N. Slinn; Mrs Spoonley, Robert Stephenson & Hawthorns; D. H. Stewart; E. E. Thomas; Thomas Wynn Thomas; Eric Tonks; Paul Towers; Oliver Veltom; G. Venables; Vulcan Foundry Ltd; L. Ward; H Watkins; G. Weaver; H. F. Wheeller; P. B. Whitehouse; G. Dudley Whitworth; E. H. Williams; J. Williams; J. Williamson; Colonel Sir Owen Williams-Wynn CBE.

In particular my especial thanks to Ifor Higgon for so generously allowing me the use of his own meticulous notes and of his extensive collection of excellent photographs, to Mike Morton Lloyd, Cambrian Steward of the Historical Model Railway Society, to many officials and departments of British Rail, to the Librarian, Keeper of Prints and staff of the National Library of Wales and to Eric Thomas for a great deal of assistance in many ways. For reading the original proofs I am most grateful to Messrs P. J. Garland and W. F. B. Price.

Introduction

A railway consists of many more things besides engines and trains. People and products and their traffic requirements called the trains into being, the loads and the countryside dictated the engine design and many supporting services had to be established before a single train could be run. The money available dictated how good the engines and trains could be and how well they and the track could be maintained; and Parliament, by Board of Trade Regulation, dictated the minimum standards required for safety, wherein so many companies were apt to fall short to preserve their profits.

Of all railways the Cambrian epitomised the struggle against all odds to adjust to the stresses imposed upon it by circumstance and to maintain itself as a going concern. Even at its best it was a total failure in producing monetary wealth for its shareholders. Its greatest riches lay in its fund of friendship, goodwill and service towards the countryside for which it carried and towards the holidaymakers it conducted to the coast. It had no great or famous locomotive prototypes which set trends in design, not did it have any ugly ones; the general run of them left an impression of workmanlike neatness and the stock list exemplified admirably the sound products of the leading private makers. By the practice of absorbing minor unprofitable branch systems, coupled with occasional shopping expeditions into the second-hand market, the Cambrian added to its own locomotive stock a collection of the most delightful examples of small tank engines to be owned by any one company.

There was besides a touch of timelessness about the Cambrian. It seemed to come from a saner world than our own. Its devotees forgave it its small irregularities, its impromptu halts at nowhere and its longer halts in the passing loops, where those going on holiday could gaze across with smug superiority at the homegoers looking with envious eyes from the other halted train. Among those countless holidaymakers it carried would be fishermen seeking peace by the beautiful rock-studded streams crossed and re-crossed many times by the line itself, walkers heading for the mountains and above all the children. To their ears the roar of braking on wheels as the coastwards train burst out of Talerddig cutting was music — an overture, perhaps, to the steady quadruple drum-beats of the bogie coaches racing down the Dovey Valley and ringing out loud and clear 'Down-to-the-beach, down-to-the-beach, down-to-the-beach'. The six-wheelers, of course, rolled out a dignified 'Soon-we'll-be, On-the-beach, Soon-we'll-be, On-the-beach . . .''

It was a long journey in terms of time but well worth enduring, for at the end lay the sea, the beach, the rocks and pools — and a high tea served by one of that great legion of landladies named Mrs Davies, Mrs Evans, Mrs Jenkins, Mrs Jones, Mrs Parry or Mrs Thomas and not forgetting Mrs Meredith, Mrs Morgan, Mrs Owen, Mrs Richards, or Mrs Lewis or Mrs Rees.

Author's note

In the 1890s a number of place-names were roughly anglicised to assist the visitors. This process has been reversed in later years and in the text the spelling and naming used is that found to be current when the photograph was taken. Also, the Cambrian had no consistent policy for commissioning official photographs. Anything we have is by pure happenstance, both in existence and in quality.

The Railways of North & Central Wales

The map shows how the rival companies had the Cambrian completely surrounded and cut off from all hopes of any lucrative through traffic. It is intended to be diagrammatic only, particularly as to the precise routes taken by the other companies. The dots represent the approximate positions of stations to convey some idea of the relative density of their local facilities. All is generally as pre-1922.

The minor branch known as the Trefonen or the Treflach went to Coed y Go and was built privately by Thomas Savin to serve his coal and brick interests. There was also a tramway from Coed y Go to the canal at Redruth. The Crickheath and other early tramways around Llanymynech and Pant, too, have had to be left off, because their tiny lengths would have confused the main presentation.

Dovey Junction, opened as Glandyfi, later became Glandovey Junction. Llanfihangel is now Llandre. Barmouth Junction only a few years ago woke up to find it had become Morfa Mawddach. Ballast Hole, Borth, and another Ballast Hole north of Tonfanau were once extra staff stations. Garth, between Arthog and Penmaenpool, was a busy little mineral siding like so many others now long

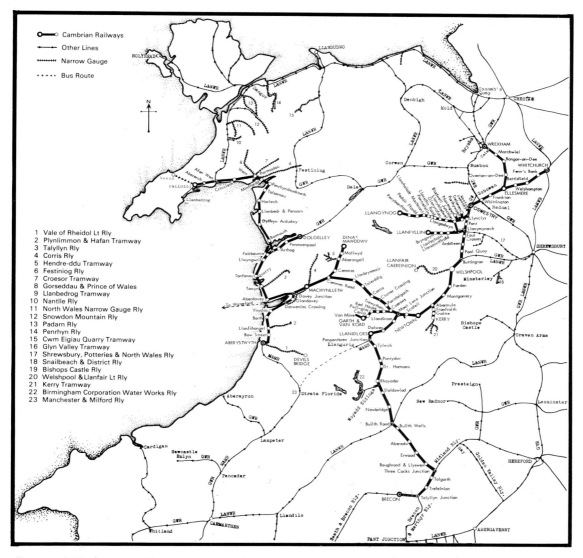

Cambrian Railways
Other Lines
Narrow Gauge
Bus Route

1 Vale of Rheidol Lt Rly
2 Plynlimmon & Hafan Tramway
3 Talyllyn Rly
4 Corris Rly
5 Hendre-ddu Tramway
6 Festiniog Rly
7 Croesor Tramway
8 Gorseddau & Prince of Wales
9 Llanbedrog Tramway
10 Nantlle Rly
11 North Wales Narrow Gauge Rly
12 Snowdon Mountain Rly
13 Padarn Rly
14 Penrhyn Rly
15 Cwm Eigiau Quarry Tramway
16 Glyn Valley Tramway
17 Shrewsbury, Potteries & North Wales Rly
18 Snailbeach & District Rly
19 Bishops Castle Rly
20 Welshpool & Llanfair Lt Rly
21 Kerry Tramway
22 Birmingham Corporation Water Works Rly
23 Manchester & Milford Rly

disappeared. The forerunner of Fairbourne, before Barmouth Bridge was opened, was aptly named Barmouth Ferry and Fairbourne itself was by local request to have been Ynysfaig. It had been built by the McDougal Estate, which had bought all the surrounding land for development under the name of Fairbourne, and the Cambrian was given the option of buying the station off the developers within five years if it proved profitable. 'Unfortunately', the locals were told, 'the nameboards have already been painted'! Unfortunately, too, it has not been possible to fit in the Soloman Andrews Tramway, of which parts became the basis of the Fairbourne Miniature Railway.

Caia by Wrexham, Wern west of Portmadoc, and Weston Wharf south of Oswestry were the Cambrian's three goods-only stations. Two minor branches, Sweeney by Weston and

Tonfanau Quarry, were only just long enough to merit the name and Cambrian engines had to proceed well off the main to work them. Besides these there were a number of sidings for special traffic, but arrangements could be made for ordinary goods at some of them.

All the terminal branches had gone out of business through lack of traffic before the Beeching closures of 18 January, 1965; and after this date only Buttington to Aberystwyth and Dovey Junction to Pwllheli remained in regular service. Of the inland stations only Welshpool, Newtown, Caersws and Machynlleth have remained open, with Borth and Aberystwyth to represent the original four 'little lines', one can still wait for one's connection at Dyfi Junction. The coast has fared better, as only Afon Wen has been lost.

From the beginning to 1857

In the beginning there were the central lands of Wales – the heartlands, as Professor Bowen has called them – with a few fertile valleys, many narrow and steep-sided ones, and many more square miles of infertile mountains. Beyond the mountains the coastal pockets were separated from one another by cliff and rock.

The people were hard-working and frugal and livings were not easily got, except on the richer soils of the wide valleys. These were held mainly by a squirearchy much given to absenteeism, which was often reflected in the run-down condition of their estates. The industrial revolution had not touched them nor would it ever alter their lives directly.

The main sources of energy were the muscles of men and horses, as few estates by then had steam engines; these and water power were more likely to be found in mines and mills. The rounded haycocks were pitched up by hand and threshing was done by hand-flail. The hilly areas supported large flocks of the small native sheep, which can prosper there having twice as many mouths to pick out the thin grasses and twice as many legs to propel the searchers per hundredweight of mutton and wool as their much larger, softer English cousins. Cattle, the ancestors of the Welsh Blacks, were numerous along all the valleys, and most households had their own milch cows.

Because of the seasonal nature of the farming and the need to find work all the year round, the hill folk combined agriculture with the search for minerals and many were both labourer and farmer besides being miners or quarry men.

Manufacture was still not prolific, being mainly production of Welsh flannel, the descendant of the home-spun 'frise of Cambria' of mediaeval times. Much of this went away by waggons along the Severn Valley or by the Montgomeryshire and Shropshire Union canal systems after it had been woven in the steam-powered mills of Newtown, which had become the main manufacturing centre.

The road system was simple, a skein of narrow ways following the valleys and connected by occasional pass-roads crossing the watersheds. Often these last were the old green ways of pedlar and pack-horse, such as Ffordd Gam Elen which is now, as it was then, a remote passage-way across the high Berwyns. The scanty coach services along these roads were adequate for the demand, as only the wealthy and the merchants could afford comfort when travelling and the rest rode in carts or on horseback – or went on foot.

Transport over the sloping fields was often by 'car llusg' – a practical and ingenious arrangement, half travois and half sledge. Because of its stable attachment to the horse's harness via wooden shafts, it avoided the dangers of over-running inherent in the man-guided sledges of the slate quarries; with them it needed only a moment's inattention for the sledge-hand to be crippled under a quarter of a ton of careering slates.

By the toiling standards of the time the area had considerable mineral wealth. In the main it left the mines by sledge and pack-horse or cart, usually in the direction of the coast, where many small sloops and brigs plied out of vestigial harbours or from as high up the estuaries of the Dyfi and of the Dysynni as they could be floated.

Traffic down the Dwyryd and the Glaslyn had ceased already with Maddock's reclamation of the

Far left: Benjamin Piercy. The able Civil Engineer to many of the little lines, his first plans for a direct line from Shrewsbury to Montgomery were stolen from his hotel during the hearing in Parliament to give the GWR and L&NWR time to bring in their joint line to Welshpool. *The Story of the Cambrian.*

Left: Sir Watkin Williams-Wynn. Almost the prototype of the professional railway director, he had *Wynnstay*, a Llanidloes & Newtown engine, named after his estate; the Oswestry & Newtown honoured him on an 0-6-0 Goods, *Sir Watkin*, and 40 years later the Great Western followed with a 4-4-0 'Bulldog', No. 3375 *Sir Watkin Wynn*, for his son. *The Story of the Cambrian.*

Below left: Mrs Ann Warburton Owen. Besides inducing the line to miss her estate by taking up £10,000 worth in shares she gave a bugle to the Railway Rifles, for which gesture an engine was to be named *Glansevern. The Powysland Museum.*

estuary by the construction of the Cob, along which ran the gravity- and horse-operated Festiniog Railway. This innovation, the 1ft 11½in. gauge brainchild of C. E. Spooner, which connected the quarries of Festiniog with the still new harbour of Portmadoc, was only a foretaste of how the new form of transport could, overnight, ruin the old and yet provide more work in other ways.

Promoters, politicians and people argued, wrangled and often indulged in bitter invective against one another for years before any part of a railway got built. The records of the proceedings before the formation of the four little companies which were to become the Cambrian provide wonderful examples of the eloquence, the wit in debate and the brilliant liveliness — '*hwyl*' — in which the people of Wales excel.

Railway companies needed individual Acts of Parliament before they could become lawful bodies with powers to buy land and build and run their lines. When their Bills were presented to Parliament by a local supporting Member they could be opposed by other Members supposedly on abstract grounds of what was best for the countryside. In fact the opposition was usually inspired by rival companies wishing to build an alternative and to secure for it the traffic expected: or wishing to prevent the formation of the proposed company because it might lessen their profits by draining off some of their traffic to perhaps a better route. So from 1836 onwards there flourished a solemn array of proposal and counter-proposal of survey and alternative route, with all the attendant legal and political machinations. Until 1853 this produced nothing other than meaningless prospectuses and the expense accounts of the professionals involved. Even then so little progress followed that the Rev. Samuel Roberts wrote a doleful letter to the Shrewsbury Chronicle to the effect that 'it was 1854 and never yet have we had the pleasure of a trip on a Montgomeryshire railway'. This was the true spirit in which the Cambrian lines were eventually conceived: it was not that they were needed and had great commercial futures, merely that the local people felt they were missing out by not having any railways.

By 1853, when the promoters of the Llanidloes & Newtown Railway got their enabling Act, the opportunity for any centrally situated railway to become a link in an important transport route had been argued away for all time. A potentially fast route for the Irish Mail via the valleys of the Severn and the Dovey or the Mawddach had been bypassed by the London & North Western's North Coast route to Holyhead on the Island of Anglesey; and the great way between Manchester and the North and the potentially great port of Milford Haven had been provided by the Great Western's taking over the Shrewsbury & Chester interests and linking with its South Wales lines via joint lines shared with the North Western. Thus two great companies separately pursued policies of watching and listening to accounts of the affairs of the little companies, of obtaining representation on the tentative boards of directors (openly or otherwise), of supporting to weaken the other's cause, and of withdrawing support when one of the little companies looked like gaining strength in its own right, all paid off. The local promoters were left with nothing but their own internal traffic and no choice other than which of the many alternative, difficult valleys the lines should take. Right from the start, the little companies had to face the situations which dogged the lines all their days and gave rise to the affectionately bestowed cognomen *'yr hen Gambrian druan'* – the poor old Cambrian.

As already mentioned, the Llanidloes & Newtown Railway was the first to get its powers. These enabled it to build a railway which had no connection with any other. Its powers to extend later to Oswestry were defeated by 1855, when the Oswestry & Newtown Railway bill received

assent. And so it went on. The Newtown & Machynlleth Railway powers followed in 1857 and those of the Oswestry, Ellesmere & Whitchurch Railway in 1861, each line competing with its neighbour for subscribers, labour and materials.

A fifth candidate for the combination which would eventually become the Cambrian was the Aberystwith & Welsh Coast Railway, authorised in stages from 1861 until it too joined in 1865. The Mid Wales Railway was authorised earlier in 1859, but 'enjoyed' an uneasy separate existence in near-bankruptcy until the Cambrian started to work it in 1888. Other separate promotions were the Mawddwy Railway in 1865, which was operated by the Cambrian from 1911, and the Van Railway in 1873, which was operated by the Cambrian from 1896.

Far left: The Reverend Samuel Roberts of Llanbrynmair. He typified the enthusiastic supporter of railways in Montgomeryshire for their own sake rather than for commercial reasons. Known affectionately as 'S.R.', he was a great social reformer and a brilliant and vehement preacher. *S. R. – Gwaith.*

Left: Earl Vane. The remoteness of the landowner from his tenants and of the Board of Directors from the railwaymen is well illustrated by this gracious portrayal of Earl Vane, later the Marquess of Londonderry, the first Chairman of the Cambrian. *S.R. – Gwaith.*

Below: Sir John Hanmer, MP. He opposed strongly the Great Western schemes to build branches from Rednal to Oswestry and to Ellesmere and only possibly later to Whitchurch. Admittedly, the Great Western scheme would have severed his estate, but without his support the northern section of the Cambrian would never have existed. *Illustrated London News.*

Directly fostered promotions which the Cambrian worked virtually from their opening were the Wrexham & Ellesmere Railway, authorised in 1885 and worked first in 1895; the Tanat Valley Light Railway, authorised in 1899 and worked from 1904; and the 2ft 6in-gauge Welshpool & Llanfair Light Railway, authorised in 1899 and worked from 1903.

The last fling in extension of the Cambrian domain was the acquisition of the 1ft 11½in-gauge Vale of Rheidol Light Railway, authorised in 1897, opened in 1902 and taken over in 1913. It was this minor addition which was to bring the Cambrian the unique distinction of owning the only surviving pre-grouping line in the British Rail system still using steam as its only service motive power.

1857 – 1864:
and a little way
beyond

Then came the contractors and their engines; and the first and greatest contractor was David Davies of Llandinam. Such was the haste of the people of Llanidloes to have their railway that the plans, sections and specifications of the two miles to Morfodion were to be inspected at 11 o'clock on 2 October 1855, the tenders were to be in by 7 o'clock the same evening and the ceremony of cutting the first sod was to be held the next day. The local man knew his ground and undercut two rivals of considerable standing. Mr Whalley cut the first sod instead of Mrs Ann Owen, who took offence because she had not been asked before the publication of a notice which said she would be so doing.

The construction advanced well, and David Davies was awarded the contracts for the rest of the Llanidloes & Newtown Railway. He built from Llanidloes to Llandinam using only men and horses, and carted all imported materials from the canal terminal at Newtown. Then in 1857 he leased the line from the company and *Dove*, the first locomotive, was dragged on 'timber carriages' over the rough roads from Oswestry. The motive power was fourteen horses, and three more engines and some rolling stock followed by the same means. True always to his strong religious principles, when one of the cortèges failed to complete its journey by Saturday night it stood in Newtown High Street until the following Monday. The line was opened formally on 2 September 1859 and was operated by David Davies.

During this period, David Davies took Thomas Savin into partnership. Comparing the value to the railways they built of these two men, it was the dogged reliability of David Davies which saved the Llanidloes & Newtown and soon after the Newtown and Machynlleth, and the brasher enthusiasm and flair of Thomas Savin which enabled the building of the Oswestry & Newtown and of the Oswestry, Ellesmere & Whitchurch. The partnership was short-lived; it was dissolved from 29 October 1860 and the two men went their separate ways. Savin was in and out of partnership with others until his bankruptcy on 5 February 1866. Much of his deficiency was represented by already worthless shares in the companies whose lines he had built, which were all he could set against his debts to manufacturers from whom he had ordered locomotives and rolling stock in his own name. Even land stood in the names of 'Mr Savin and his Inspectors'. His reckless driving on with the Aberystwith & Welsh Coast route before negotiations with landowners were completed, brought lawsuits and compensation payments galore. By such intermingling of his own finances with those of the companies, he assumed the right to use engines wherever he wished regardless of the location of the nominal owning company. Small wonder, then, that an earlier writer should assume that a list of engines he found was the Cambrian stock list; in fact, it was either Savin's own list of the engines he was using or at best a first offer to the Cambrian when his complex affairs were being unravelled.

Another partnership, Watson and Overend, took on the job of completing the Mid-Wales Railway, the second of the early 'outsiders' which would eventually join the Cambrian. They also made the mistake of accepting shares and securities as payment for their work, but otherwise the Mid Wales, too, could never have been built.

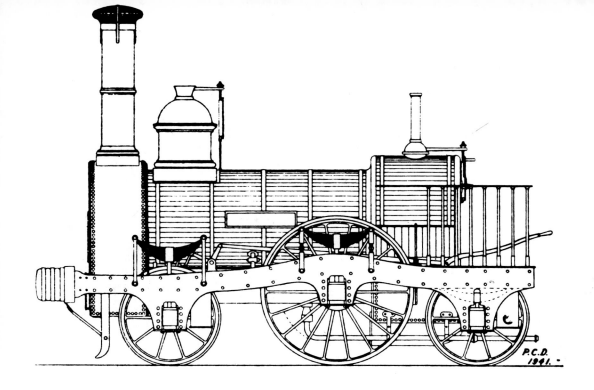

Top left: David Davies. The able and forthright teetotal Calvinist Methodist 'top sawyer'. He ventured first into construction, then, as 'Davies the Ocean', he became one of the great coal-owners. He professed to be a graduate in the 'University of Observation'. *National Library of Wales.*

Above: Dove, Sharps No.55 of October 1839, ran originally on the Birmingham & Derby Junction Railway for whom she made trouble by being 'out of gauge' when run on London & Birmingham rails. She did little better for David Davies and her working pressure of only 55 lb per square inch made her a doubtful buy. *The Locomotive Magazine.*

Right: Thomas Savin. The 'small haberdasher' who rose to be a 'railway king', then fell into bankruptcy, all within ten years. His mistaken way to power was to accept too many shares in lieu of payment for work on lines which could never pay. Without such an idealistic contractor few of the lines which became the Cambrian would ever have been built. *Top Sawyer.*

13

Above: The Sharp Stewart saddle-tank *Milford* was bought by David Davies to complete the Llanidloes & Newtown and arrived by horse traction to be isolated around March 1859. Originally she had no cab and water was fed into her boiler by a steam donkey-pump. Probably she was sold to the Cambrian when David Davies went on to coal mining. *Collection C. C. Green.*

Below: The first locomotive venture of the Lilleshall Iron Company bore their Works No.1, and appeared in the London Exhibition of 1862. Savin bought her in December 1863. She became Cambrian No.21, Ballast Tank Engine, and was sold in 1868. *The Locomotive Magazine.*

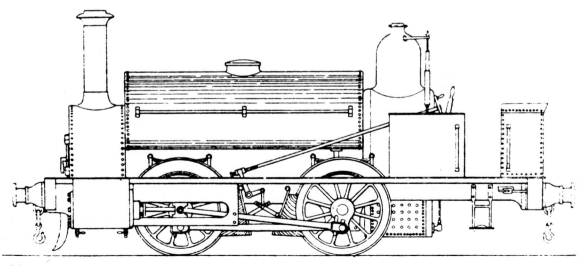

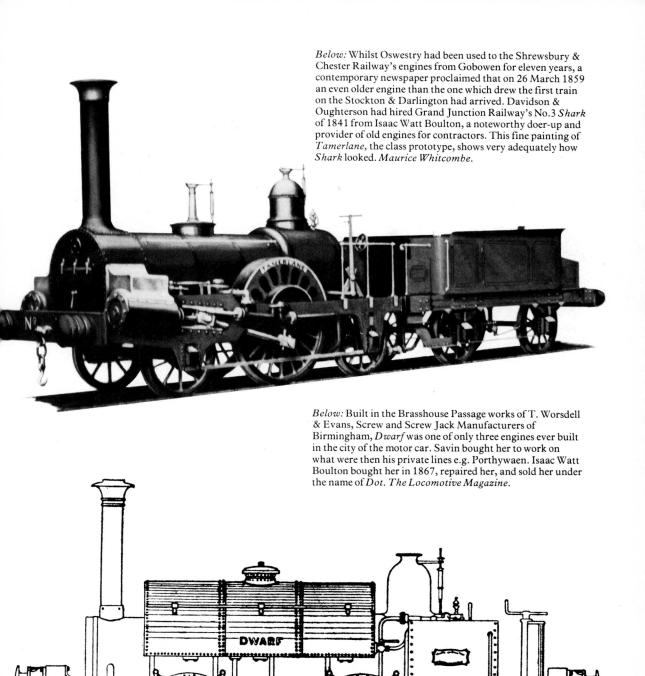

Below: Whilst Oswestry had been used to the Shrewsbury & Chester Railway's engines from Gobowen for eleven years, a contemporary newspaper proclaimed that on 26 March 1859 an even older engine than the one which drew the first train on the Stockton & Darlington had arrived. Davidson & Oughterson had hired Grand Junction Railway's No.3 *Shark* of 1841 from Isaac Watt Boulton, a noteworthy doer-up and provider of old engines for contractors. This fine painting of *Tamerlane*, the class prototype, shows very adequately how *Shark* looked. *Maurice Whitcombe.*

Below: Built in the Brasshouse Passage works of T. Worsdell & Evans, Screw and Screw Jack Manufacturers of Birmingham, *Dwarf* was one of only three engines ever built in the city of the motor car. Savin bought her to work on what were then his private lines e.g. Porthywaen. Isaac Watt Boulton bought her in 1867, repaired her, and sold her under the name of *Dot. The Locomotive Magazine.*

15

Above: Safe ashore after her tow across the Dovey in a barge from Ynyslas, behind the steamer *James Conley,* Thomas Savin's *Merion* poses with her footplate crew on Aberdovey quay as the fist engine to get there. With Cardigan she ran the train services north until the line from Dovey Junction was completed. The Class 1 Manning Wardle saddle-tank featured prominently in the construction of the lines which became the Cambrian and six passed into Cambrian stock after the sort-out of Thomas Savin's bankruptcy. *Enterprise* (known as the 'Black Donkey,) became Cambrian No.1 and had been hauled by road (as were *Dove, Squirrel* and *Milford*) to work on the isolated Llanidloes & Newtown. David Davies bought *Llandinam* in 1861 for his work on the Newtown and Machynlleth. Savin bought another eight, of which five (including one bought from Brecon & Merthyr funds), became Cambrian Nos. 13 *Whixhall,* (re-named Green Dragon) 14 *Nantclwyd,* 17 *Merion,* 18 *Cardigan* and 24 *Borth. Pioneer* and *Hereford* became Brecon & Merthyr's *Blanche* and *Lady Cornelia* respectively, and *Usk* kept her own name until the Brecon & Merthyr acquired a second *Usk,* after which the older engine got dubbed *Little Usk.* The Cambrian classed their six as 'Ballast Tank Engines' until this work was belatedly completed. All were sold by 1875.

There was also a four-wheeled Class 4 Manning Wardle tank called *Tiny.* Ordered for the Hereford, Hay & Brecon, *Tiny* was 'diverted' into the Cambrian area and worked Savin's own coal trains.

Besides hiring of engines for constructional work and short-term chartering of steamers, such as the *James Conley,* a passenger-carrying paddle steamer named the *Elizabeth* was chartered for a much longer term. This was used to ferry passengers from trains propelled down the curving bank from Ynyslas to a quay on the east bank of the Leri. The shunt and the crossing to Aberdovey took only 33 min, a time which was never equalled by the replacement rail connection along the north shore of the Dovey Estuary. When the new all-rail connection from Machynlleth was completed it became known as 'The Doveyation'. *J. Parry.*

Above right: No. 16 in the 'mystery' list, this Manning Wardle 0-6-0 of 1862 went into Brecon & Merthyr stock as that company's No.6. She was named after the Brecon & Merthyr's Chairman, John Parry de Winton. The Cambrian ordered six similar engines in 1866, but could not afford them, so the makers sold them, four to the Taff Vale and two to the London Brighton & South Coast. Another Manning Wardle tender engine, an 0-4-0, became Cambrian No 2. At least eight more engines have been traced as having worked for the contractors. *National Library of Wales.*

Right: In 1863 the *Illustrated London News* marked the completion of the third of the little lines with this engraving. The temporary nature of the station is evident, but under construction beyond it is the engine shed which lasted to the end of steam. *Illustrated London News.*

The look of the early railways

The character and appearance of each of the little railways form a delightful and interesting collection of diversities. Their backgrounds were some of the loveliest countryside that one could possibly wish to see. The 'stage props' — cuttings, embankments, abutments and bridges — were planned by Benjamin Piercy with considerable forethought to use as much local material as possible — as little as possible was to be brought in at greater cost. Stations and other buildings followed suit, but often were not completed until the line had been running for a year or two — or even longer.

Top right: Dolwen, a typical single-storey station of the Llanidloes & Newtown. It was run by one of the Cambrian's very few station mistresses, Miss Anne Jenkins. As a little girl six years old she would have seen the arrival of the great modern invention — the railway train — and she lived right through its best years until 1936. *C. C. Green.*

Below: The bridge at Morfodion where David Davies started to build the first stretch of the Llanidloes & Newtown. It has survived in its original form to carry British Rail. The Llanidloes & Newtown had an easy route with only five problems in bridging; timber by canal barge to Newtown was the solution. *C. C. Green.*

Centre left: The Oswestry & Newtown was the second of the easy routes and Thomas Savin had to build only two major bridges. This one crossed the Vyrnwy. Benjamin Piercy's triple caissons, built for the second track which never materalised, and plugged with mass concrete and banded to prevent their cracking apart, carried British Rail's replacement welded girders to the end. *C. C. Green*

Below: Most of the original timber station buildings on the Oswestry & Newtown were replaced in various forms of brick and stone, but Llanymynech survived to show us both the open shelter and the timber booking office of the period. *C. C. Green*

Left: The Kerry Branch of the Oswestry & Newtown ascended the charming Mule Gorge. It was designed for single line only. The near arch crosses the river. This is a scene at Fronfaith, c 1905. *Collection C. C. Green.*

Bottom left: In a road overbridge at the East end of Newtown station, the Oswestry & Newtown gave the Cambrian its earliest example of the Brymbo Foundry's 'bulb-headed' cast iron plate girders. Others came later when the Cambrian had to replace its many unprotected road crossings with sloping ramps and bridges. *C. C. Green.*

Top right: One of the several fine bridges between Talerddig and Cemmes Road. *C. C. Green.*

Centre right: The single-line Llanfyllin Branch of the Oswestry & Newtown provided the Cambrian with one of its two 'flag' stations. Unless an intending passenger hauled up the arm showing the white disc on the red arm to the oncoming train it would not stop. The guard restored the signal. *Courtesy of M. E. M. Lloyd.*

Below: Designed by Piercy and George Owen, this splendid bridge near Cemmes Road marked the end of the difficulties of constructing the Newtown & Machynlleth and the last major use of stone taken from Talerddig cutting. The draining of the Carno bog, the crossing of the watershed and the descent of the Twymyn Gorge had been accomplished – and Davies the Contractor had arrived. *C. C. Green.*

BRYNGWYN RAILWAY STATION.
"You work the Signal to stop your Train."

Top left: The Coast section's most troublesome stretch – the Friog cliffs. The ledge, it is said, was cut by sailors who could stand the heights above the rocks and surf; the men of Borth and Derwenlas, whose ships had just been laid up to rot, would have been glad to have the work. The overturned coaches were derailed in the Friog accident of 1883.
Powys Area Library Newtown.

Centre left: For most of his railway bridges, Benjamin Piercy had evolved a standard design – 8in square baulks of timber bolt-hung from the bottom flanges of wrought iron girder sides. This bridge across A4083 outside Whitchurch was built in 1862. Daylight can be seen through the spaces between the beams. *C. C. Green.*

Bottom left: Typical of the stone station buildings of the Newtown & Machynlleth – Llanbrynmair at the turn of the century. The stationmaster's cap on the boy's head was prophetic, for Mr. W. R. Fryer was to retire as stationmaster of the station where he was born. Then nearly all young boys in rural areas wore frocks which could be handed down to the next youngest boy or girl. *Courtesy of W. R. Fryer.*

Above: The Oswestry Ellesmere & Whitchurch produced little drama in its construction. Having no stone, the idiom was brick as used in the station buildings at Bettisfield. Where its over-bridges stood on Sir John Hanmer's estates they bore his arms. *C. C. Green.*

Below: Before the Aberystwyth & Welsh Coast joined the Cambrian Thomas Savin managed to complete the isolated stretch from Aberdovey to Barmouth Junction and the Dolgelley branch as far as Penmaenpool. The road bridge was built by a private toll company which the Cambrian bought out after 1900. *G. Hayward.*

1859-1864:
Early Locomotives
and Rolling Stock

Below: Thomas Savin ordered six of these Sharp Stewart goods engines in his own name for the Oswestry & Newtown: *Queen* (the class name), *Prince of Wales, Hercules, Vulcan, Tubal Cain* and *Cambria*. David Davies ordered six for (to quote the makers) 'The Newton and Mackynnleth', named *Talerddig, Countess Vane, Sir Watkin, Cyfronydd, Rheiwport* and *Towyn*. Ten arrived between December 1861 and February 1863. *Rheiwport* and *Towyn* were delivered to the infant Cambrian in August 1864. All had Monsieur Giffard's new patent injector systems. *G. Grundy for Sharp Stewart.*

Bottom left: Thomas Savin's last order was for ten 2-4-0 passenger engines from Sharp Stewart. *Mazeppa* was the first to arrive at Oswestry in March 1863, followed by seven others – *Pegasus, Albion* (the class name), *Minerva, Cader Idris, Glandovey, Plynlimon* and *Rheidol*. The other two were lost to the Brecon & Merthyr. Four were delivered in March 1863 and four in March 1864. So that all the details showed up well, an engine was usually photographed for the makers in its matt grey undercoat with the maker's own lining also in matt paint, but only on the side to be photographed, as in this view of *Albion*. After this ceremony the proper colours were applied. *G. Grundy for Sharp Stewart.*

Top: Three of these fascinating little Sharp Stewart tanks were obtained by Thomas Savin, nominally for the Llanfyllin, Porthywaen and Kerry branches of the Oswestry & Newtown, in June 1863. Although depicted here around 1890, *Prometheus* has no ownership plate and apart from the

trace of lining on the cabside looks very much 'as delivered'. The other two were *Plasfynnon* and *Mountaineer*. *Locomotive Publishing Co.*

Above: Six Sharp Stewart 0-4-2 engines were ordered for the Llanidloes & Newtown. Four, named *Montgomery, Llanerchydol, Leighton* and *Volunteer* (the class name), stayed in their proper area, but *Wynnstay* and *Glansevern* were lost to the Brecon & Merthyr in Savin's bankruptcy. Three were delivered in 1859, of which only *Montgomery* ever got to Llanidloes a year later when the isolated line was joined on to the Oswestry & Newtown; the other three followed at the end of 1860. Hearsay memories have it that the colour was a dark green. *Collection C. C. Green.*

Top right: This three-compartment first-class coach at Coney Crossing, Oswestry, was one of the rare contenders for the title of centenarian; it can be taken as typical of the small four-wheeled coaches of the original companies. *C. C. Green.*

Centre right: At 21 ft 6 in long, this Ashbury second-class coach did not give much in the way of legroom. Built in December 1860 for £287 it became a sleeping van in 1920 and achieved the distinction of surviving briefly in Great Western ownership. *J. P. Richards.*

Below: This 25 ft 6 in long first- and second-class was bought from Ashbury's in February 1861 for £387. Converted to a parcels van in 1915, it was condemned on sight by the Great Western as from 10 September 1922. Seen here in Herbert Jones' livery on 21 July 1904 as part of the royal train lent to Birmingham for the opening of the Elan Valley Waterworks by His Majesty King Edward VII. *L&GRP.*

Far right top: Evidence of the comfort provided for the gentry from the outset: four-wheeled first-class saloon with twin-door luggage compartment at the nearer end and a separate compartment at the further end for the servants. *G. H. W. Clifford.*

Far right bottom: The footplate crew had only wood-blocks on the tender-wheels with which to check speed and every train had to have three or more of these 'break-vans' (as they were then called). Each guard had to watch constantly from his ducket for emergency signals from in front or from behind. Note the floor-level square door leading to the dog box; dogs were not allowed in the carriages. *J. E. Cull*

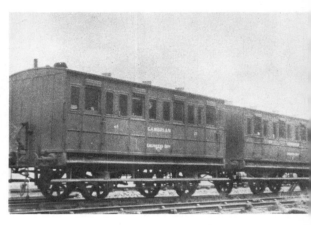

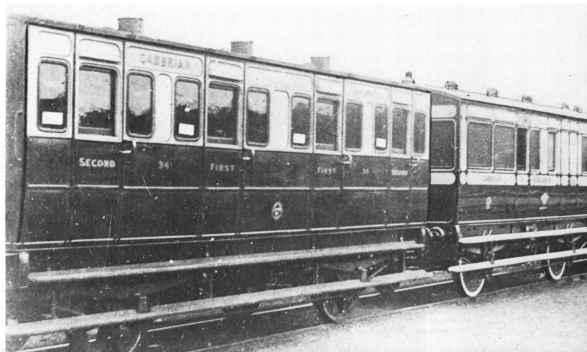

1864 – 1885: Birth of the Cambrian Railways

The Cambrian Railways Company obtained its powers to combine and run the original four little companies on 25 July 1864. The Aberystwyth & Welsh Coast was unable to comply in time with Parliamentary Standing Orders, but it had completed its first bit of line as far as Aberystwyth five weeks before. The tenor of the first directors' report was that, whereas hitherto the aggressive policies of the great companies had always done more harm than good, from now on the new company was to be run for the benefit of its shareholders, which would also be for the benefit of the public. The principal opponent of the bill for amalgamation had been the Great Western and the new company worked in closer co-operation with the London & North Western.

After making a hefty cash contribution to aid the construction of the Aberystwyth & Welsh Coast and agreeing to operate it, the Cambrian absorbed it on 5 July 1865. By the following February Thomas Savin was bankrupt and three months after that Overend and Gurney's Bank, the greatest negotiating organisation of its time, also collapsed. The struggle to recover scattered rolling stock from the Savin empire and to complete the Coast route now began. As settlement

Below left: Mr. W. W. E. Wynn of Peniarth, Towyn is reputed to have designed the company's armorial device. By omitting the letters 'C.R. Co.' from the three dark semi-circular areas this version was evolved. It was applied to carriage sides as an ownership embellishment by William Aston some time after 1882, date of the first proven evidence of bronze-green and white, lined gold on a wider black band, as the official carriage livery. *Courtesy of George Dow*

Below: Two relics of 'The Scheme'. The initials on the ticket stand for Oswestry & Newtown and Llanidloes & Newtown Railways; the label reads Oswestry & Newtown & Llanidloes & Machynlleth Railways. Beautifully engraved copperplate letterheads of the Oswestry & Newtown and Llanidloes & Newtown Joint Railway are also known to exist. *Courtesy of W. G. Bett and Collection C. C. Green*

Right: Penhelig in 1868. The recently-built embankment and road bridges, both of the underhung timber deck type, and No.4 Tunnel indicate the completion of the link with the rest of the Cambrian from Dovey Junction to Aberdovey Station on 14 August 1867, and the end of the *Elizabeth's* ferry service. *Courtesy of Mrs. C. F. Ellis.*

Bottom right: The men who managed the Cambrian at first.
Standing centre: Mr George Owen the Engineer, formerly assistant to Benjamin Piercy during the construction, 1864-98.
Standing right: Mr. Henry Cattle, Traffic Manager, 1870-1878.
Seated left: Mr. Alexander Walker, Locomotive Superintendant – formerly superintendant to Thomas Savin's varied locomotive stud, 1866-1879.
Seated centre: Mr George Lewis, Secretary & General Manager, 1864-1882.
Seated right: Mr H. C. Corfield, Solicitor. *The Story of the Cambrian.*

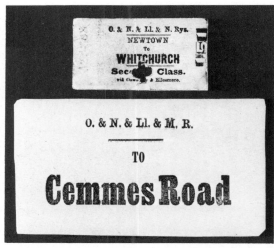

O. & N. & Ll. & N. Rys.
NEWTOWN
To
WHITCHURCH
Second Class.
via Oswestry & Ellesmere.

O. & N. & Ll. & M. R.
—
TO
Cemmes Road

proceeded and engines were conceded beyond dispute to the Cambrian, one can imagine the satisfaction with which the little brass plates with blue infilled grounds reading 'CAMBRIAN RAILWAY No. etc.' were affixed.

The odds were too great and the new company went bankrupt on 15 February 1868, with the deputy-chairman Captain Robert D. Pryce as receiver. What was known as 'The Scheme' kept things going uneasily until the 'old constitution' was restored on 1 January 1879; then matters finally collapsed and the Cambrian was bankrupt again on 12 July 1884. This time an able and ruthless professional, John Conacher, who had been secretary since 1882, took over as receiver. He reduced no less than seventy different forms of stock to ten and re-organised the capital liabilities down to under £6 million. The main trouble was on paper, for as a working railway the Cambrian was not doing too badly, so he was able to satisfy the creditors and get the company discharged from bankruptcy by 18 February 1885.

Above: The stations of the Coast route were mainly of wood and several were replaced by brick. Dyffryn Ardudwy is typical of the latter. Note the water-proofed roughcast and tile-hung gable – attempts to make the house more habitable in westerly gales. *C. C. Green*

Below: The principal feature of the coast route, the original 'cock-and-draw' or 'overdraw' bridge across the Mawddach channel close to Barmouth. The gentleman who knew the bridge could not be built, and swore to eat the first engine to cross it, was dumped down at a table in Barmouth and asked if he wanted it roast or boiled – possibly some time in October, 1867, when a proper train service replaced a leisurely horse-drawn carriage that had worked since 3 June that year. *Collection C. C. Green.*

Top right: No. 45 *Rhiewport* came in for an odd treatment of the ownership marking – 'CAMBRIAN RAIL CY' on the centre splasher and No. 45 on the leading splasher. With No. 46 *Towyn* she was delivered to the Cambrian direct only a month after the company had been formed – perhaps this

was the reason. Like the six Newtown & Machynlleth engines, she has a six-wheeled tender. Later these were swapped about with the four-wheeled tenders according to working needs. Two more, Nos. 51 *Snowdon* and 52 *Harlech*, arrived in 1865. A further four Nos. 1 *Victoria*, 2 (soon renumbered 4) *Alexandra*, 6 *Marquis* and 10 *Marchioness* were added in 1872/73. *Locomotive Publishing Co.*

Right: Sharp Stewart goods No. 27 *Cambria* at Machynlleth c 1870, now painted in unlined black; only the brass plate above the centre axle proclaims that it belongs to the new Cambrian. The other eleven had become Nos. 11 *Queen*, 12 *Prince of Wales*, 19 *Hercules*, Brecon & Merthyr 3 *Vulcan*, 26 *Tubal Cain*, 34 *Talerddig*, 35 *Countess Vane*, 39 *Sir Watkin*, 40 *Cyfronydd*, 45 *Rhiewport* and 46 *Towyn*. *Locomotive Publishing Co.*

Bottom right: No 30 *Albion* with her plate of Cambrian ownership. The other seven had become Nos 28 *Mazeppa*, 29 *Pegasus*, 31 *Minerva*, 41 *Cader Idris*, 42 *Glandovey*, 43 *Plynlimon* and 44 *Rheidol*. *Courtesy of Ifor Higgon.*

Above: An inaugural present for the infant Cambrian – eight of these London & North Western style first/second composites already on order were delivered in July and August 1864. No. 76 was to run until the Great Western detected her in September 1923; at least they photographed her before she was scrapped. She is seen here at Blodwell Junction in post-1899 livery. *L&GRP.*

Left: Built by the Midland Wagon Company around 1864 for £62.50, this dumb-buffered wagon survived until 1900. A new wagon took its number in 1904. *Cambrian Official.*

Bottom left: The brigantine *Charlotte* of Aberdovey (Thomas Daniel, Master) painted entering Leghorn in 1864. The directors feared that red and green railway signal lamps could be mistaken by the navigators of these beautiful little ships for the port and starboard lights of other vessels, so causing them to be wrecked through standing too close inshore. Cambrian railway signal lights were therefore violet for danger and white for all clear. *Courtesy of Mrs C. F. Ellis.*

Right: Guard Cudworth. Right through to the 1890s the servants who directly attended the public bore collar patches of identification – 'PORTER' or 'GUARD' and senior staff wore the silver feathers emblem. *The Story of the Cambrian.*

Below: The Cambrian took four more Sharp Stewart passenger engines at the end of 1865. Nos. 53 *Gladstone*, 54 *Palmerston*, 55 *Treflach*, and 56 *Whittington* were a new departure in naming, two being national politicians instead of directors or their homes. See how carefully the jet pilots of their day have groomed their machine for its photograph with symmetrical rag-dabbing on the tender and side-sheet. Oswestry, c 1870. *Courtesy of Ifor Higgon.*

Top right: Oswestry, 1870. This photograph merits close study. The six wagons in the background rake are: (from left to right): an outside-framed sprung buffered wagon, with traces of small lettering; a dumb-buffered drop-door wagon with no trace of lettering; a similar, slightly higher wagon with traces of small lettering; a short box wagon with three words along the second plank down; a vehicle similar to the second wagon, but definitely lettered with three words, centrally; and a sprung low-sided wagon loaded with rough stone. On the extreme left is a dumb-buffered Cambrian two-plank, fixed-side wagon, which was shunted into place during the lengthy time exposure (about two minutes) that was needed to create the image on the slow wet plate. The first of the nearer pair of wagons carries a tarpaulin lettered 'CAMBRIAN RAILWAY 507'. The wagon on the extreme right is a Cambrian drop-side with raised ends. The four-wheeled box-van is one of the 'break-vans' delivered in 1864 by the Metropolitan Railway Carriage & Wagon Co. The five-compartment outside-framed Parliamentary (the term was just about still in use, as evidenced by a timetable of the time) third is another acquisition of 1864 from the Metropolitan Carriage & Wagon Co. 'Compartment' is a nominal term only, for the divisions ceased at seat level. Here the number looks like 86 in a plain garland. The colour is probably brown. Under the end of the timber a short dumb-buffered fixed-side wagon is serving as a match-truck. *Courtesy of Ifor Higgon.*

Below: 2-4-0 No. 43 *Plynlimon* poses with an outside-framed five-compartment Parliamentary third, an open interior four-compartment third, a first/second composite, an outside-framed three-compartment Parliamentary brake third and a sliding-door roader parcels brake-van. The other engine is 0-6-0 No 6 *Marquis*. Aberystwyth, c 1875. *Courtesy of Ifor Higgon.*

Above: No 42 *Glandovey* with the crude tongued and grooved-board front and sides fitted to the spectacle plates in the 1870's to give a little protection to the crews. There were still no roofs to form even elementary cabs. Seen at Barmouth, c 1888. *Collection C. C. Green.*

34

Above: In May 1866 three of a new sort were received from Sharp Stewart & Co, Nos. 57 *Maglona*, 58 *Gladys* and 59 *Seaham*. Note the dumb-buffered wagon and the intriguing fragment of an outside-framed open but roofed cattle truck. Llanfyllin, c 1890. *L&GRP.*

Below: Sharp Stewart 0-6-0 tank No 13, bought in February 1875 for banking duties between Machynlleth and Talerddig. It was decided that she should henceforth bear the name of her place of work and 0-6-0 No 34 *Talerddig* gave up her nameplates and received a grander pair , *Cader Idris*, which were lying spare in Oswestry works. This had been brought about by the realisation that the name and title of the chairman's wife was borne by – *a goods engine!*

Accordingly, 0-6-0 No 35 *Countess Vane* was downgraded to *Castell Deudraeth* and the 2-4-0 passenger engine No 41 *Cader Idris* took the title, the company thereby purging itself of *lése majesté*. No 13 ended her days as the Workshop Engine at Oswestry until 1920, after 45 years of service, with little alteration besides the new chimney and steel brake-blocks. Even then her service was not finished, for her boiler went to raise steam for the Aberystwyth pumping station and her frames and motion were bolted down inside Oswestry Works to drive additional machinery.To the last, Oswestry wasted nothing. *Locomotive Publishing Co.*

Above: No. 59 *Seaham* halted at Vrondirion near Dolgelley, c 1882. The leading van is Oswestry & Newtown brake No. 101 lettered 'PASSENGERS LUGGAGE'. The second coach is an Ashbury-built 1st/2nd composite No 47 and is still carrying an earlier device on a shield-shaped mounting. The remaining coaches are Cambrian outside-framed Parliamentary stock of 1864. Colours are probably cream and|brown *John Thomas; Courtesy of The National Library of Wales.*

Top right: In August 1878 two of a new class to become known as the 'Small Sharp Stewarts' were delivered. They were virtually extended and improved 2-4-0s, and the rebuilds of the latter were strongly reminiscent of their new cousins in outline. These were the first engines to carry the company's device and the last to be given valence-mounted ownership plates and names, which were those of great statesmen – Nos 16 *Beaconsfield*, seen here at Oswestry in 1891, and 17 *Hartington.* Eight years elapsed before the Cambrian could afford two more, Nos. 20 and 21 (the Cambrian's first vacuum-braked engines), and Nos. 50 and 60 followed thirteen years later in 1891. *Locomotive Publishing Co.*

Centre right: William Aston reported in 1882 that cabs similar to those fitted to 'the new engines' could be made in the works for £13 and these were added as engines came into Oswestry for other work. This haphazard method of selection caused the job to spread into the 1890s. *The National Library of Wales.*

Right: The new livery, probably introduced by William Aston as his first change around 1882, was black with a light blue-grey lining flanked both sides with equally wide signal red – a rather flamboyant style. It is seen on Sharp Stewart goods 0-6-0 No. 12 *Prince of Wales.* Within the previous three years the company had taken on three more of this type, all bargains. Sharps had built them in 1875 for the Furness, which could not afford them, so in 1878 Sharps offered two as unused for £1,765 each, barely half what they would have cost if ordered new. These became Nos. 14 *Broneirion* and 15 *Glansevern,* and at last Mrs. Ann Warburton Owen had her long-promised named engine. The third Furness 'reject' went to the Denbigh Ruthin & Corwen Railway, which soon became London and North Western property. She was later offered to the Cambrian, who bought this, their final example of the design, for £1,125 in 1879 and made her No. 18 *Orleton.* In 1879, too, Alexander Walker retired and William Aston became Locomotive Superintendant. *Cambrian Official.*

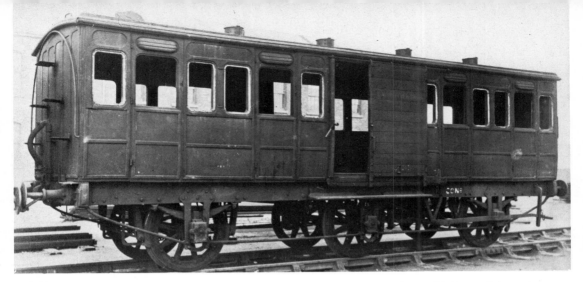

Above: In 1882 the first two six-wheelers were built in Oswestry Works. They were 28ft 6in long five-compartment thirds, costing £300 each. More followed next year, built by the Metropolitan Railway, Carriage, and Wagon Co. for a lower price of £260 each. One of the first pair, No. 116, was made into a parcels van in 1918 and appeared in the Great Western's 'rolling museum' series of photographs taken in 1923. *GWR Official.*

Below: No. 37 *Mountaineer,* with the new lining and Cambrian Railway ownership plate. The other two of this type became Nos. 36 *Plasfynnon* and 38 *Prometheus.* *Locomotive Publishing Co.*

Above: Dolgelley train at Barmouth Junction in the early 1880s. The locomotive is a Sharp Stewart 0-4-2 of the 'Volunteer' class running tender-first. The first coach is an outside-framed parliamentary brake-third with plain instead of birdcage roof; the second is a first/second composite of 1864; and the third is a four-compartment third. The last is a very intriguing specimen indeed. It has the oval-panelled doors of the three-compartment first at Coney Crossing pictured earlier and was possibly first-luggage – first-first; it is still in one of the early overall brown liveries. *Collection G. Dow.*

Below: The first of the Cambrian's three 'classic' accidents – the Friog of 1 January 1883. About 30 tons of stones and soil from the toll road above fell on to the track and overturned No. 29 *Pegasus* onto the beach. The driver and fireman were killed, but the leading coach – the outside-framed coach on its side above – was empty and most of the passengers in the four-vehicle train were in the third coach, which never left the rails. *Collection C. C. Green.*

1885 – 1899: The Cambrian grows up

The build-up to a high standard of smartness and service now began. First, the carriage stock had to be upgraded to attract passengers to make holiday journeys to the coast. That meant more of the new six-wheel thirds for a start, and some new luggage locker composites for through running. More goods stock was acquired too. Now the years of attrition were over. The locomotives and carriages were greatly increased in number and much improved in standard and appearance.

Above: Alfred Aslett, General Manager from 1891-1899 – a conscientious autocrat who carried on the process of improvement started by Connacher. *The Story of the Cambrian.*

Left: One of the two men who set the Cambrian to rights – John Connacher, the ruthless professional who was Secretary from 1882 and General Manager from 1890. He went to the North British Railway as General Manager in 1891, but came back to the Cambrian as Chairman, 1909-1911. *The Story of the Cambrian.*

Above: No. 1 *Victoria* before 22 April 1886, resplendent in a trial lining of red edged blue-grey. *Courtesy of Ifor Higgon.*

Below: Mid-Wales Kitson 0-6-0 No. 12 at Newbridge-on-Wye. The lame duck that the Mid-Wales had become was taken over in 1888. The Cambrian acquired ten of these worn-out lightweights and managed to concoct four runners, which were numbered 25, 32, 33 and 47. Only No. 33, combining Mid-Wales No. 7's frame and No. 8's boiler, lasted past 1895 to be scrapped in 1904. The livery at first was dark green and the lining, which curves in at the corners, was said to have been broad black edged gold: with the beautiful lake-terra cotta hue of the carriages, the Mid Wales when new must have looked magnificent. *Courtesy of Ifor Higgon.*

Top: Mid-Wales Kitson 0-4-2 No. 2 of 1864 outside Builth Wells Stores with her new oval cast brass number plate, slightly smaller than the old one, now reading Cambrian Railways No. 2. Originally there were six of this type, of which four came to the Cambrian as Nos 2, 22, 23 and 24. All were scrapped by 1905. The single curved lining, probably gold, was the Mid-Wales' last livery. Old Cambrian memories recalled that she was painted black, but one instance of an 0-4-2 in brick-red was recorded by H. Holcroft. *Cambrian Official.*

Above: Mid-Wales Sharp Stewart 0-6-0 No. 9 at Llanidloes about 1885. She and her sister No. 10, built in 1873, became Cambrian Nos 48 and 49 as additions to the 'Queen' class – the best engines the Cambrian gained out of the takeovers. The livery shown here may have been dark green or even plain black. *Courtesy of Ifor Higgon.*

Right: The Mid-Wales bridges were devised so that all could be assembled from only eleven basic components. The spidery multi-span ones, fine for the light Kitson engines and short trains, gave much trouble later on; all had bracings added and many had to be encased in solid concrete piers to arrest their downstream 'creep'. The middle of 'Q' bridge across the Ithon was noticeably further to the west than its ends before it was dismantled. This is 'A' Bridge over the River Dulas. *C. C. Green.*

42

Above: The route to Brecon was scenically one of the loveliest runs any railway had to offer the traveller, winding as it did along the steep-sided valleys of the Dulas, the Marteg and the Wye. This is 'N' Bridge over the River Wye, south of Rhayader. *C. C. Green.*

Below: By 1888 the old quay at Aberdovey had been much improved and it is interesting to see the outer rail running within a foot or two from the edge. The brig *Excelsior* is unloading timber into Cambrian wagons about 1898. *Courtesy of J. Parry.*

Top: This fanciful print of two steam brigantines, one flying the Dragon of Wales at the jackstaff, some old advertising notices, and a book of cabin tickets have survived to mark the Cambrian's short-lived venture into shipping with the *Liverpool* and the *Cambria* in 1889. By getting the afterguard of the *Liverpool* drunk, so that they mistook Cardigan Bay outer buoy for the inner and lost a tide, thereby necessitating the slaughter of an entire boatload of thirst-crazed cattle on Towyn beach, the London & North Western agent at Waterford put paid to the Aberdovey and Waterford Steamship Company within a few months of its first sailings. A second attempt with a better ship, the *Magnetic*, which was succeeded by the *Electric*, also failed. *Collection C. C. Green.*

Above: The second pair of Small Sharp Stewart 4-4-0s, Nos 20 and 21 (seen here at Oswestry in March 1889), were delivered in July 1886. The lighter colour of the tender sheeting is an illusion caused by rag-dabbing. The device on the leading splasher was to become a constant feature on the passenger engines from now on. *Collection C. C. Green.*

Below: No 53, ex-*Gladstone*, at Oswestry in March 1889. Mr Aston had set about improving both the appearance and performance of the little 2-4-0 passenger engines. The Sharp Stewart choker chimneys were scrapped and his new chimneys improved the blast and steaming. Brakes on the engine as well as on the tender were worked by vacuum and required an injector pipe along the boiler into the smokebox,

so the nameplates had to go. To compensate, the leading splasher has been sheeted over to carry the device. *Locomotive Publishing Co.*

Top: No. 54 ex-*Palmerston* also in renovated condition at Oswestry in March 1889. With the blue-grey lining edged signal red and all brasswork polished the 'Albion' class now cut quite a dash. E. L. Ahrons wrote in his series on 19th century railway working that he had difficulty in understanding how the Cambrian maintained its services. The returns for 1888 showed an *average* working day, locomotive and crew, of 13 hours, with only two engines at a time in works for lengthy repairs. *Locomotive Publishing Co.*

Above: No 9 ex-*Volunteer* at Oswestry in March 1889 with a proper cab and an Aston chimney, vacuum and steam brakes

working on the driving wheels, and steam sanding – the only one of her class to attain all four refinements. With No 8 (ex-*Leighton*) she was scrapped in 1899. The other two of the class No 5 (ex-*Montgomery*) and No 7 (ex-*Llanerchydol*) went four years earlier. *Locomotive Publishing Co.*

Below: In December 1888 No 15 ex-*Glansevern* emerged from the works with a new boiler on a higher centre-line and working at a higher pressure. In this form 16 of the old 'Queen' class became invaluable little machines of considerable versatility. As yet she still has brakes on the tender only and gravity sanding, but she bears the first cast-brass number plate to replace her valence-mounted ownership plate. Seen here at Oswestry in March 1889. *Locomotive Publishing Co.*

Top: No. 48, one of the Mid-Wales Sharp Stewarts, was the second to be 'done up' in March 1889. However, the goods engines must have been kept strictly to such duties as they still had no engine brakes. The Ramsbottom safety valves which were to become standard on the Cambrian show more clearly here. *Locomotive Publishing Co.*

Above: No. 6 *Marquis* at Oswestry in March 1889, still with only her matchboard weather protection. Some of the class had these fitments added between 1885 and 1888, but others received proper cabs as their first improvement. Note the elaborately panelled lining on the tender. *Locomotive Publishing Co.*

Top right: No. 51 *Snowdon* at Oswestry in March 1889. Her nameplates were removed before the month was out following a general policy decision to abandon names on locomotives. *Locomotive Publishing Co.*

Centre right: 'Queen' class No 52 *Harlech*, at Oswestry around 1889, shows an unusual arrangement of nameplate and makers plate. *Courtesy of Ifor Higgon.*

Right: Montgomery Station c 1890, with an 'Albion' class 2-4-0 on a London & North Western train. Also seen is original wagon No. 1067 with dumb-buffers, in light grey with black iron-work and solebars. *John Thomas, Courtesy The National Library of Wales.*

Top to bottom: Llanfihangel geneu'r Glyn, later Llandre, c 1890, with a 'Queen' class 0-6-0 on the right. Already an early four-wheeled coach has been 'grounded' by the station as a store of some sort. The private owner wagons are: Lewis Edwards No.2; dumb-buffered Rd. Williamson & Sons No.134; and William Morgan No.3 *John Thomas Courtesy The National Library of Wales.*

A posed scene of the period, taken at Towyn in 1891. The train is even placed on the wrong line so that the glare from the sea on the right is assisting and not hindering the cameraman. Note the covered-in state of the rails – as yet there is no foot-bridge. The end window reads 'SECOND CLASS WAITING ROOM' *Courtesy of Mrs. C. F. Ellis.*

In 1890 Nos 56 ex-*Whittington* (seen here at Oswestry in 1891) and 31 ex-*Minerva* were the first of the 'Albions' to receive the new higher-pressure boilers similar to those fitted to the 'Queen' class; the 'Albions' got steam sanding as well. Despite shorter chimneys, they still retained their dashing look. *Locomotive Publishing Co.*

No 1, formerly *Victoria*, at Oswestery in 1891. She did not lose her archaic look until rebuilt in 1893. Nobody seems to have raised any objection to the name of the reigning monarch gracing a goods engine. *Locomotive Publishing Co.*

Above: Ellesmere Station provided offices for the Oswestry, Ellesmere & Whitchurch and later for the Wrexham & Ellesmere Railways. Here, in 1892, the Cambrian made its mark in the annals of trade union history. John Hood, the stationmaster, had given evidence before a Parliamentary Committee enquiring into over-long hours worked by railwaymen (a 60 hour working week was nothing unusual and only the Welsh regard for Sunday observance kept the hours worked from being even more). He was sacked and for this breach of privilege the Chairman, General Manager, and Board were publicly admonished by the Speaker at the Bar of the House of Commons. The Secretary of the Amalgamated Society of Railway Servants of the United Kingdom denounced the Cambrian, saying that 'little railways were a gigantic mistake', and the Labour press thundered 'Cambrian Tyranny'. But such was the power of management in those days that Mr Hood stayed sacked. Later he achieved a long career of honourable public service in local administration at Ellesmere. *C. C. Green.*

Below: No 4, formerly *Alexandra*, after 5 May 1891. She was the fourth of the Sharp Stewart 0-6-0s to be modernised with a new boiler – and then they became really up-to-date. Exhaust ejector pipes and six-wheel brakes have also been added. *Locomotive Publishing Co.*

Below: Any one of these engines would have worked Noyadd Sidings from Railway No.1 of the Birmingham Corporation Waterworks. In order they are *Elan, Coel, Calettwr, Rhiwnant, Nant Gwyllt* and *Claerwen.* All were built by Manning Wardle & Co., except for *Nant Gwyllt,* which was a Hunslet. Two more Hunslets, *Methan and Marchnant,* were mostly working away at the top end of the valley – sometimes even cut off when tracks were severed and re-aligned. All took their names from streams which flow into the reservoirs. Noyadd Sidings, just south of Rhayader Tunnel, were worked by Cambrian engines which delivered construction materials for the reservoirs and took away empty wagons; the Birmingham engines returned the empties and took away the full on the last stages of their tortuous journeys. The engines were kept from meeting by an agreed time embargo. *Courtesy of J. Hamer.*

Bottom right: A close-up of *Coel,* which according to Manning Wardle was assembled from standard parts off a written specification without a drawing. The gentleman on the right is G. N Yourdi, the Graeco-Irish Resident Engineer. His 'saloon' is an ex-Mid-Wales brake-van. *Courtesy of Birmingham Water Dept.*

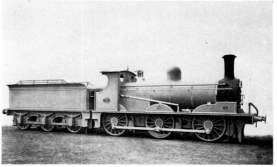

Top left: A pause from shunting duties at Minfford about 1891. *Queen* has lost her nameplate and, unlike the rebuilt engines, probably had not changed in appearance any more when she was scrapped in 1899. The embankment behind carried the narrow-gauge Festiniog Railway and the track against the bank on the right served the Maenofferen Slate Quarry exchange sidings on top of the bank. The diminutive trucks were worked into position for unloading via a grid of tiny turntables. Behind the camera the track curved down to form three parallel sidings leading to the goods shed. The line coming away to the left past the signal served first the coal-drops, whence the Festiniog received its supply of prime-mover fuel, and then descended in a long curve to get alongside more narrow-gauge exchange sidings. The main line is down out of sight behind the signal. Altogether Minfford was a difficult station, both for halting a train and for shunting. *Courtesy of Ifor Higgon.*

Centre left: An Aberystwyth-bound local train at Machynlleth in the early 1890s with an 'austerity' Oswestry-built third class coach leading, then a diminutive saloon composite with an end-luggage compartment, another third and a six-wheeled brake third. The 'Albion' class 2-4-0 is still unrebuilt except for a cab, covered-in wheel splasher and a new chimney. One envies the photographer the full-hearted co-operation of the assembled station staff and passengers. *J. Thomas, Courtesy of The National Library of Wales.*

Top right: In 1893, with only six reasonably new engines out of a total stock of 59 – and of these a further 17 badly needed rebuilding and nine were past it – Mr. Aston brought out his 61 class, later known as the 'Large Sharp Stewarts'; 20 were delivered in the six years to 1898. Nos 61-68 were delivered in 1893 in various experimental liveries, which were soon discarded, but the 1894 batch, Nos 69-72, showed a fresh

arrangement; there was a device only on the splasher and a cast brass numberplate, both items which were thereafter standard. The pronounced lead of the bogie, well in advance of the main weight of the cylinders and boiler, made the 61 class very steady runners and they were esteemed very highly by their crews. *L & GRP.*

Above: In 1894 Nos 73-77, the first five of these handsome little engines, were delivered by Neilson Reid & Co. who delivered two more, Nos 87 and 88, in 1899. They took their designer's name and became the 'Aston Goods'. Unlike those of any other Cambrian engines, their sand-boxes were faired into the leading splashers; Nos 78-80, built by the Vulcan Foundry in 1895, had much larger ones. *Neilson Reid & Co.*

From	Times of Starting	Third Class Fares there and back.	
		DAY TRIP	THREE DAYS
	dep.	a.m.	
Pwllheli	,,	6 0	
Afon Wen	,,	6 15	
Criccieth	,,	6 21	
Portmadoc	,,	6 30	
Minffordd	,,	6 34	**6s.** **10s. 6d.**
Penrhyndeudraeth	,,	6 38	
Talsarnau	,,	6 42	
Harlech	,,	6 50	
Llanbedr and Pensarn	,,	6 58	
Dyffryn	,,	7 8	
Barmouth	,,	7 20	
Town	,,	7 50	**5s.** **9s. 6d.**
Aberdovey	,,	8 0	
Aberystwyth	,,	9 0	
Bow Street	,,	7 50	
Llanfihangel	,,	7 54	**10s. 6d.**
Borth	,,	8 0	
Ynyslas	,,	8 4	
Glandovey	,,	8 14	
Machynlleth	,,	9 50	
Cemmes Road	,,	8 43	**5s.** **9s. 6d.**
Llanbrynmair	,,	8 53	
Carno	,,	9 10	
Pontdolgoch	,,	9 20	**5s.** **9s.**
Caersws	,,	9 26	

Left: A faded and stained excursion bill of this period found in the roof of Barmouth Junction. *Collection C. C. Green*

Below: The old smithy at Oswestry works. The two steam hammers at the back were supplied to the Oswestry & Newtown Railway and as late as 1964 it was still possible to lay hands on a huge spanner marked O & N. Although relatively small, these works had rebuilt all 12 'Albions', 16 of the 'Queens' and the three Seaham tanks between 1890 and 1897. *E. Colclough.*

Top right: This early Kodak snapshot taken about 1895 of No 37 *Mountaineer* at Abermule, shows hazily the author's uncle enjoying a brief moment of a small boy's dream. More important, it shows the round-topped opening, closed by two half-flap doors, in the cab rear through which coal was handed down from the Kerry branch coal-store – a wagon parked against a buffer-stop in Abermule. *Courtesy of S. D. Moore.*

Centre right: William Aston's 0-4-4 tanks, built by Nasmyth Wilson & Co, were neat effective units which served well both on the Wrexham and Ellesmere and on the Dollgelley branches, often moving quite heavy trains on these short hauls. Nos 3, 5 and 7 were delivered in 1895 and 8, 9 and 23 in 1899. No 5 is seen as new, running in 'broad Aston' livery. Note the 'ISCA FOUNDRY, ENGINEERS, NEWPORT MON' plate on the turntable undertruss, and the oil lamp on the right and the addition of the neat little tool box. *Courtesy of R. E. Thomas.*

Bottom right: The second of the Sharp Stewart 2-4-0 tanks to be handsomely rebuilt, No. 59 *Seaham* (named for the chairman's son, Viscount Seaham) figured in this official photograph of 1894. It has new boiler, Aston chimney, Ramsbottom safety valves, steam sanding and a full lining-out. *Cambrian Official.*

Above: On 11 June 1897 the Cambrian had the second of its 'classic' accidents, when a Sunday School excursion returning to Royton after a happy day at the seaside left the rails at Welshhampton. The company maintained that the leading van, a Lancashire & Yorkshire four-wheeler, was running rough. The van's owners declared indignantly that anything would run rough on Cambrian track. Colonel Yorke, the Board of Trade inspector, found the track to be in an inadequate condition for fast running and that 11 children had been killed in a tumbling, sliding disorder which should never have happened. More young lives could have been saved if some of the wreckage could have been raised only a little, and as part of its expiatory actions the Board of Directors ordered that henceforth all engines should carry heavy lifting jacks. *Courtesy of Paul Tims.*

Right: In August 1896 the company started working the Van Railway (opened in 1871) and so once again had Manning Wardle saddle tanks on the strength. Van Railway No 2 of 1877, became Cambrian No 25 and the older No 1 of 1871 Cambrian No 22, but being in poor condition the latter was scrapped only three years later – and to confuse the record No 22's ornate Doric safety valve column was put on to No 25. Ex-Van Railway No 2, now Cambrian No 25, is seen in the broad Aston livery at the Van Mine about 1898. The collection of free ballast from the old mine spoil-heaps proved a disaster; the metallic ore dusted badly and before it had finally settled it would badly grind away a low-slung valve-gear's brass bearing metal. After that the engineer's department had to be more careful about selection and use. *Courtesy of W. R. Bradley.*

Centre right: The Van carriages were no assets – of the two this was the better one. It is unlikely that either ran much after 1893 when the line became derelict. Pwll-glas had the typical station-cum-crossing keeper's house and signals, seen here in 1908. In its prime the Van lead mine was rich and profitable, but the Cambrian did not take over the railway until all this was in the past. *G. M. Perkins.*

54

Top: Welshpool on 25 June 1896 as No 68 takes over the Great Western Royal Train, standing at the London & North Western platform to take Edward, Prince of Wales, to Aberystwyth for installation as Chancellor of the University. *Courtesy of Ifor Higgon.*

Bottom left: Four more Class 61 came from Sharp Stewart in May 1895 as Nos 81-84, but the last four of the class, Nos 32, 47, 85 and 86, were built by Robert Stephenson & Co. and were delivered during 1897 and 1898. Note the larger Stephenson plate now on the leading splasher. *Real Photographs.*

Above: An Aston bogie tricomposite carriage at Barmouth in 1898 in Aston's dignified bronze-green and white livery with black banding and central gold stripe round all the panel mouldings. The two devices proclaim that it belongs to the Cambrian Railways. Detailed examination of the over-exposed negative reveals that the compartment wording on the doors is three thirds, two seconds, and one first and that the coach is No 274. As yet 'CAMBRIAN RAILWAYS' does not appear on the panels above the windows. The route board reads 'CAMBRIAN RAILWAYS MANCHESTER BARMOUTH' in red, with some unreadable gold lettering in the middle – probably 'THROUGH CARRIAGE'. *L&GRP.*

Far left: Signals controlling main-line movements had Chance Bros. 'ruby-gold' glasses for danger. Fine gold-dust in the glass gave a ruby violet effect as in Victorian wine-glasses, classed in the rule-books as violet. The all-clear aspect was plain white glass. Shunt arms had pale magenta glass which photographed white. All-clear for shunt movements was pale green. These signals are at Llynclys Junction. *L&GRP.*

Left: A typical Cambrian gantry construction at Barmouth Junction North Box, surviving in 1918 as built except for the 1914-18 wartime replacement of pale green for all-clear on the main-line arm. *H. W. Burman.*

Far bottom left' A typical Cambrian point indicator lamp at Llanbrynmair. The aspects were pale green for set straight and 'ruby-gold' or magenta for set to turn. *C. C. Green.*

Bottom left: Signals with arms slotted into the post were being replaced by the orthodox externally-pivotted arm type. Tall signals in exposed sites had wound-up lamps to save climbing. The Cambrian never departed from the painted disc on signal arms, except on distants, which bore an acute fish-tail stripe. *H. W. Burman.*

Above: Aston's last six-wheeled carriages, brought into service in 1899, appeared from the works in C. S. Denniss's new brighter livery. This is brake 3rd No 78. *Cambrian Official.*

Below: A typical warehouse crane at Llanbrynmair. Note triangulation of support up in the roof beams. *C. C. Green.*

1899 – 1914: The Best Years

The Best Years had come. 1899 was the end of an era; the old Cambrian men had all retired and William Aston left in that year, tired and ill from frequent brushes with the old General Manager, Alfred Aslett. C. S. Denniss, the new General Manager, brought in as Locomotive Superintendent Herbert Jones, who would support him in his drive to publicise the Cambrian and the seaside resorts it served.

CAMBRIAN RAILWAYS.

THROUGH LAVATORY CARRIAGES

BY

Special Service of Express Trains,

RUN AS UNDER:

LONDON (Euston)
To Aberystwyth via Welshpool 9 §30, 11 0 a.m.
and 2 35 p.m.
To Barmouth via Welshpool, 9 30 and 11 0 a.m.
To Criccieth via Welshpool, 9 30 and 11 0 a.m.

LIVERPOOL (Lime Street)
To Aberystwyth via Whitchurch, 8 15, 10 30,
a.m., 12 10 and 3 25 p.m.
From Aberystwyth via Whitchurch, 8 45 a.m.,
12 5 noon, and 2 15 p.m.

☞ GREAT ACCELERATION
Between **Leeds, Sheffield,**
LIVERPOOL, MANCHESTER,
and other LARGE TOWNS in
LANCASHIRE AND & YORKSHIRE
ABERYSTWYTH, BARMOUTH,
AND THE
Cambrian Coast.

Top left: Charles Sherwood Denniss, the forceful and publicity-conscious General Manager who made every effort to make the Cambrian a popular and paying railway. *The Story of the Cambrian*

Far left: Herbert Edward Jones, the locomotive superintendant who helped Denniss to cut costs; the old perfectionist ways of William Aston had to go. Occasionally Herbert Jones' enthusiasm for his craft ran away with him, as one delightful story testifies. Going to a conference of the Institute of Mechanical Engineers he entertained two fellow-travellers who joined him at Reading with a dissertation on railway matters in general and on the art of designing locomotives in particular. It was only on arrival at the meeting place that it became apparent to him that his

courteous listeners were the famous Great Western designers William Dean and George Jackson Churchward. *The Railway Magazine.*

Left: A. J. Collin, MICE, a competent and qualified civil engineer who only stayed three years, His successor, G. C. MacDonald, stayed with the company until 1922. *Commerce.*

Above and top: Today some of Denniss's publicity would be open to mischievous *double entendre*. The Victorians were much too dignified and satisfied with their efforts to detect such possibilities. *Collection C. C. Green*

Above: Literally 'mouthwatering prices' – until one
remembers the going rate of pay of 7 old pence (a little under
3p) per hour for an unskilled labourer and 1s 3d (just over
6p) for an artificer. The price for a lunch basket went down
to 2s 6d (12½p) by 1915. *Collection C.C. Green.*

Right: The wide range of pre-printed tickets held at
Cambrian stations makes an interesting study. *Courtesy of
W. G. Bett.*

Bottom right: Besides its own internal luggage labels, the
Cambrian printed very many exotic outsiders and its label-
racks must have been enormous. *Collection C. C. Green.*

Below: Denniss and Jones' first innovation was a new livery.
For the engines it meant a lining of middle chrome yellow
edged fine signal-red. The device remained on the splasher as
before, but a magnificent crest, the Prince of Wales feathers,
appeared on the tender, boldly flanked 'CAMBRIAN
RAILWAYS' in yellow shaded right and below in red. The
liberal application of fine red picking round the valences,
axle-guards and wheels is not revealed by the blue-sensitive
slow plates used by Mr Charles Thomas, who was appointed
official photographer to the company in 1899. *Cambrian
Official.*

EUSTON STATION. L&N.W.R.

Above: This elegant scene at Euston at the turn of the century shows (extreme left) an Aston tricomposite through carriage. *Raphael Tuck & Sons.*

Left: On 28 July 1900 the old Barmouth over-draw bridge was rolled back for the last time and the Cleveland Bridge and Engineering Company replaced it with the revolving bridge. *Collection C. C. Green.*

Top right: The addition of the Birmingham waterworks to the rota of work for small tank engines was causing problems by leaving only one spare. So No. 22, a standard H type Manning Wardle, Works No. 1523 of 30 June 1901, was bought for £1,100. In 1916 she was sold for war service for £700. At a capital depreciation rate of about £25 per year she must have become one of the most economical workers on record. *Cambrian Official.*

Centre right: At first, Herbert Jones repeated his predecessor's excellent carriage designs, but decked them in resplendent style in keeping with the new engine livery. The gold lining became middle chrome yellow flanked by fine red picking lines; 'CAMBRIAN RAILWAYS' in gold shaded right and below in blue appeared in the top panels, with the feathers as central emblems. The key colours remained bronze-green and white. *Metropolitan RC&W Co Ltd.*

Bottom right: The Tylwch smash, 16 September 1899. Both vehicles were in the restrained Aston livery and re-appeared a few months later in the more showy style. Seen clearly is the gas-piping on top of coach No 266, built by Ashbury's the year before for £1,020. *Courtesy of S. Humphries.*

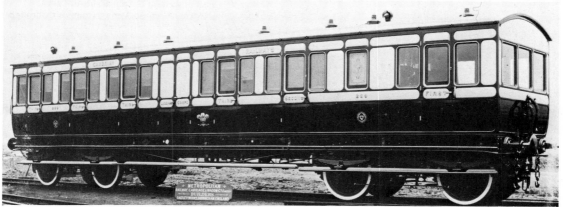

Above: On 31 July 1901 the Oswestry Works turned out No 19, a 4-4-0 generally to the standard Aston-'Large Sharp Stewart' design, and this inspired C. S. Denniss to have a publicity photograph taken of a train built entirely in the company's own works. It was taken at Llanymynech, probably in August, 1902. The six-wheeled passenger brake-vans were No.185 leading and No. 184 at the rear, both completed in 1900. The six first, second and third class (tricomposite) carriages, each with a separate lavatory reached via an internal semi-corridor for each class and having a luggage-locker at the one end, were the latest in comfort and style for through running over other companies' lines. The leading carriage was No 279 and the other five were Nos 278 and 280-283, all newly out of the works in July 1902. The tender was makeshift, as No 19's proper tender did not emerge from the works until 1903. Seemingly C. S. Denniss had grown impatient for his publicity picture and ordered the painting up for the occasion of one borrowed from another engine. Just above the rear of the tender can be seen the girders of the underdeck bridge which carried the Llanfyllin old line across the canal. *Cambrian Official*

Below: No 19's chief advance was its single-lever action twin-sliding firebox doors instead of the old oval single-flap type. There was a little 'cheating' in the claim that the engine was Cambrian-built, for Nasmyth Wilson made the boiler and firebox unit and the steam-chest; together with the wheels, these were already all in stock. *Cambrian Official.*

Below: The 'Kerry Donkey' just before the three old four-wheeled saddle tanks were replaced by something more modern. A year or so before this picture was taken, a boy of 14 tried to wreck the train by putting an obstruction across the rails. He was sent to prison for six weeks – *with hard labour. Courtesy of R. E Thomas.*

Above: By the water tank at Kerry, It was necessary to edge along the side of the wooden tank to hand the leather 'trunk' over to the filler hole, then hold the valve lever down by hand while the water flowed. *G. M. Perkins.*

Above: The Afon Leri 'Cut' was completed about 1901. This work re-aligned the river to flow directly from Borth to a new exit on the Dovey estuary, thereby draining the marshy area behind Aberleri (now the golf course) and obliterating Borth Harbour and its sea approach. The picture shows Sands Sidings and the cattle pens built for the hoped-for Irish trade before the Leri Cut was made down the opposite foreshore. The schooner is the *Volunteer* (D. Jones, Master) and the tiny gaffsail boats are the ferries operated by father and son John and Edward Bell. *Courtesy of John Burman.*

Centre right: On 4 April 1903, after 39 years of narrow-gauge schemes and counter-proposals, the Cambrian started running passenger services for the 2ft 6in gauge Welshpool & Llanfair Light Railway, using locomotives and stock 'designed' by Herbert Jones in conjunction with Beyer Peacock and R. Y. Pickering & Co. This scene shows *The Countess* on a mixed train at Castle Caereinion in the same year. Her stablemate was *The Earl*. Welshpool & Llanfair stock followed the parent company in its livery and its subsequent alteration. The W&L passenger 'station' was at the edge of the main Welshpool goods yard. *Courtesy of Tom Aldridge.*

Right: Until 1908 all Cambrian goods and passenger brakes had signal red ends. This 13-tonner left the works in December 1902. Two windows and a large removable panel were fitted into the other end. *Cambrian Official.*

66

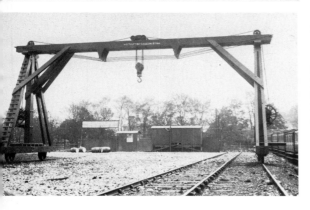

Above: In April 1903 R. Stephenson delivered the first of Herbert Jones' 0-6-0 goods engines, the class which took his name as 'The Jones Goods'. Generally they were a very effective design, marred by one major fault which was to show itself fairly frequently, and they lasted in service as well as their predecessors the Aston Goods. Nos 89 to 93 all had good-sized cabs, but the roof was still short of covering the entire footplate. The blemish of the design was that the balance-weights were all in the wrong sectors of the driving wheels; thus the 'Jones Goods' had a disconcerting habit, when running light, of developing a violent rocking motion and hopping off the track at medium speed. Legend has it that one driver dug his trackside allotment on the Saturday, regarded it with satisfaction on the Sunday and cut his bean trenches at 4 ft 8½ in centres with his engine on the Monday. Fortunately most of the mishaps with these engines were only minor ones. *Cambrian Official.*

Centre left: The works could also turn their hand to skilled fine coachwork, as exemplified in this trim-looking parcels van, c 1902. *Cambrian Official.*

Left: The 8-ton crane made by Kitchen of Warrington for Llansaintffraid was re-erected in 1902 at Spion Kop timber yard. Just how many turns of the 'steering wheels' operated by men standing on the platforms level with the carriage waist-line were required to raise the loads is not known. *Cambrian Official.*

67

Above left: On 5 January 1904 the Cambrian started working the Tanat Valley Light Railway, entirely with Cambrian locomotives and rolling stock, the Sharps 2-4-0 tanks being the usual motive power. Llangynog terminus is seen about 1905, looking down from Rhiwarch Quarry. Berwyn Granite Quarry, formerly the Llangynog Lead Mine, is in the background. *Courtesy of T. Jones.*

Below left: An official inspection party had travelled to Llangynog before the opening in the Directors Saloon (No.9) and the similar No.10, drawn by the contractor's engine – Strachan No.7. *Courtesy of M. E. M. Lloyd.*

Above: Strachan was also giving the local people free trips to the main line in his wagons to help to get them used to the idea of train travel. One lady watched a goods train go by in awe-struck silence and turned to her friend. 'Blodwen!' she cried, 'what a wealthy man that Cam Rys must be to have his name on all those wagons!' Or so an old Cambrian man related. The wagon shown was the company's maid-of-all-work, the 10 ton drop-sided, two-plank slate truck. No 927 was built in Oswestry Works in October 1899 at a cost of £65.50. *Cambrian Oficial.*

Below: Cambrian vans were painted light neutral grey, relieved by black on the outer faces of the external framing. Occasionally the sliding doors jammed through warping, but more often because the load had 'walked' across the floor. The picture is dated 21 March 1904. *Cambrian Official*

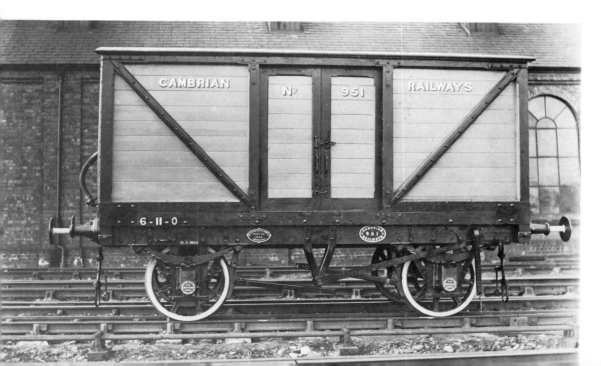

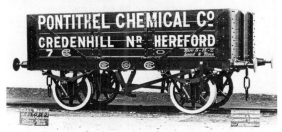

A miscellany of Cambrian-domiciled private owner wagons

Top: Photo dated 1871. Courtesy of Historical Model Railway Society

Above left: Photo dated c 1885. Courtesy of M. E. M. Lloyd.

Above right: Photo dated c 1897. Courtesy of Historical Model Railway Society.

Below: Photo dated c 1910. Courtesy of C. Meehan.

Top right: Photo dated c 1910. Courtesy of M. E. M. Lloyd.

Centre right: Photo dated c 1920. Courtesy of J. P. Richards

Bottom right: Photo dated c 1925. Courtesy of H. B. Evans.

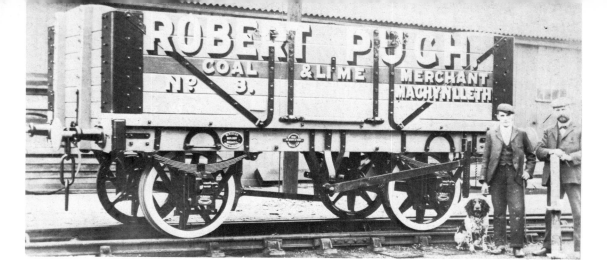

Right: In June 1904 goods trains to Oswestry conveyed the best bargains any railway had from the second-hand market—three efficient tank engines in good order for £2,000 the lot. They went straight into service in their blue Lambourn Valley livery plus cut-out brass number plates. This is Hunslet No 811 of 1903, formerly *Eadweade. Cambrian Official.*

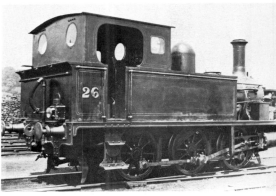

Centre right: Chapman & Furneaux No 1161, formerly *Eahlswith.* The Great Western's quick, low-price sale was inspired by a wish not to take on any engines not of Swindon design – they were then happily in ignorance of what was to come their way in 1922, including a few of their own back. *Aelfred,* a similar engine, became Cambrian No 35. *Cambrian Official*

Below: Also in June 1904 Oswestry Works completed the first two of Herbert Jones' excellent corridor tricomposite carriages. Even the Great Western ran them for nearly 30 years after taking them over. *Cambrian Official*

Far right top: On 11 July 1904 Oswestry turned out their second 'Large Sharps'-type engine, No 11. She had to wait nearly four years for her proper tender. Seen here south of Harlech on the royal staff train on 14 July 1911. *H. W. Burman.*

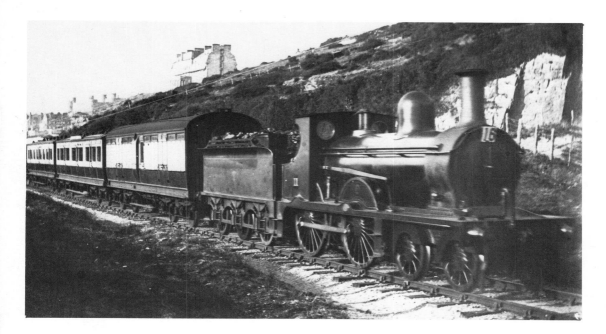

Below: At the opening of the Birmingham Corporation Water Works on 21 July 1904, King Edward VII and Queen Alexandra travelled in the Directors Saloon and *Calettwr* was fitted with a spark-arrester for the occasion. Shropshire Light Infantry and police guarded the track all the way from Rhayader. The royal train was preceded (officially) from Rhayader by three trains of beautifully dressed officials and VIPs – all sitting in slate-wagons behind engines without spark-arresters. With their finery flying in the wind, two trains' loads got away, if a bit late, but the third's occupants were still sitting loaded as the royal train was due and got shunted. The royal train left 25 min late because it got stuck at the top of the grade and had to have assistance from a Corporation engine as well as from the reserve Sharps, 4-4-0 No 82. So the third train occupants never saw the ceremony and had to be content with the luncheon. That day Rhayader dealt with 91 train movements including one which was kept in orbit between Doldowlod and Builth Wells because there was no unoccupied siding in which to put it. Of the journey in Cambrian slate-trucks Birmingham reporters wrote: 'The trip was thoroughly enjoyed and the spasmodic behaviour of the chain-coupled trucks on each occasion on restarting was productive of much merriment'. *(The Post)* 'A terrible and nerve-shattering trip and the passage of a long tunnel left the bright raiment of the ladies covered with dirt and every throat parched by sulphur fumes'. *(The Chronicle)* 'Trucks packed with mayors, generals, bishops and gaily-dressed ladies started with a jerk which precipitated every one into his neighbour's arms'. *(The Mail)* And of the time keeping – or lack thereof: 'The King was somewhat annoyed by the eccentric hours of the railway company. '*(The Mail)* Even the company's own trainload of bigwigs from Oswestry was late. *Fox-Davies – L & GRP.*

Below: When recording the effects of the head-on 'bump' at Forden on 26 November 1904, the good Mr Thomas dropped the oldest 'clanger' known to photographers. He put his glass-plate into the holder with the emulsion to the back, and reversed his picture. The accident, in foggy weather, was caused by the driver of No 47 over-running signals set at danger because the stationmaster was having horses unloaded from a goods train that was blocking the line, whereas he should have put the goods train into the proper siding. *Cambrian Official*

Above: On the same day that the Cambrian management was having such an anxious time at Rhayader, Stephensons completed No. 94, the first of Herbert Jones' own design of passenger engines. Known as the 94 class, or Stephenson 4-4-0s, they were handsome engines and their performance was good for the difficult line they worked over. Five were built, Nos 94-98, all arriving in 1904. This official photograph of No. 95 was taken at Oswestry late in 1904. *Cambrian Official.*

Top right: Sharps 2-4-0T No 59 about 1905. *Courtesy of R. E. Thomas.*

Centre right: Sharps Goods 0-6-0 No 15 at Llanymynech on the Blodwell Junction train. The tender carries a diminutive spectacle plate to provide some shelter when running to the terminus. Another useful 'evidence' picture – the tender rear panel is still lined. *L&GRP.*

Bottom right: Encouraged perhaps by the success of his second-hand shopping expedition for the Lambourn Valley tanks, Herbert Jones fell for six of Metropolitan Railway's bargain offers. 'Fell' was the operative word, as their high axle-weights and their low coal capacities and hill-climbing performances restricted their use eventually to light local and yard pilot duties. They could just manage to be of some assistance as banking engines up the Talerddig incline. No. 2 was once Metropolitan No 10 *Cerberus.* The other five were Nos 12, ex-11 *Latona;* 33, ex-12 *Cyclops;* 34, ex-13 *Daphne; 36, ex-15 Aurora,* and 37, ex-66 (un-named). *Cambrian Official*

Above: After 1867 the Cambrian had given facilities at Llan|idloes and Aberystwyth to the Manchester & Milford Railway. It also exacted payment, which in the case of Llanidloes was truly an exaction — only one train ever got as far as Llangurig, after which the creditors seized the rails and had them sold. In 1906, when the Manchester & Milford's operation between Aberystwyth and Pencader was failing financially, the Cambrian made attempts to get it, but this decrepit line was 'the one that got away', it was leased to the Great Western in that year and Aberystwyth got a foretaste of the future when two 'Dean Goods', numbered 9 and 10 were shedded there. This picture shows M&M No. 10 at Aberystwyth in 1906. *Courtesy of Miss Nichol.*

Below: Llanidloes Station about 1905 — an extremely valuable photograph for modelling detail. Note: a ventilator cover for the full width of the 6 ton van in the short carriage-truck bay; the shunt and starter signals to South Yard Neck bracketted on to the warehouse; the point indicator lamps; the small Mid-Wales shed behind the Down Home signal; the Mid-Wales goods brake with 'verandah' at each end; and the liberal use of single-slip diamond crossings. The engines on shed are a 4-4-0 'Large Sharp Stewart' and an 0-6-0 Sharp Stewart Goods. The two ladies in the left foreground are staff of Spiers & Ponds, the refreshment concessionnaires at all principal Cambrian stations. *Courtesy of R. E. Thomas.*

Left: This ingenious mobile test rig for the new water-raising pumps and their driving engine enabled the machines to be moved easily to their permanent building and gives us a close look at an old dumb-buffered timber bolster wagon. The panels on the valve-box ends bear the wording 'MAKERS CAMBRIAN RAILWAYS OSWESTRY WORKS 1906' – such was their pride in their workmanship. *Cambrian Official.*

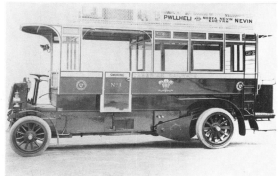

Centre left: While C. S. Denniss tried to get motor-buses for the Cambrian in 1901 he was unable to start a service between Pwllheli and Nevin until two Swiss Orion-chassis vehicles with bodies by Moss & Wood were delivered on 9 June 1906 for £770 each. The two cylinders were horizontally opposed fore and aft, separately water-jacketted and with a huge fly-wheel under the driver's seat. A vee-belt drove a circulating pump in a tank and pipe-coil cooling system visible below the door, and an extremely long, heavy 'silent'-toothed belt drove a massive gear-box to be seen below the feathers emblem. A chain-drive on either side imparted the final drive to the solid back-axle and the wide rear wheel-rims each took two tyres side by side. *Cambrian Official.*

Below: No. 22 on a train from the Van mine, about 1905. *Collection C. C. Green.*

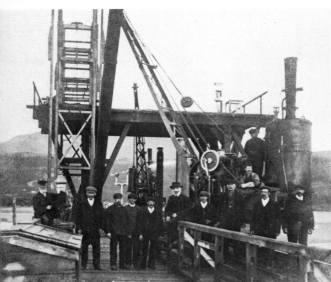

Above: Aberystwyth shed. The three even-arm bracket signals were outer homes indicating which route was open towards the platforms and the raised walkway enabled ticket examiners to clear a train before it drew in, with obvious saving in time. The shunt arms again show the pale magenta for danger. *Cambrian Official.*

Left: Between 1906 and 1909 Abraham Williams of Aberdovey rebuilt the wooden trestle section of Barmouth Bridge. Toll charges for using the timber-floored walkway had to be paid *at both ends*, once for entering and once for leaving, ie a lady in a bath chair paid 1d for herself, 1d for the pusher and 1d for the chair four times over if she actually left the toll way at the other end and then returned. *Courtesy of T.I. Hughes.*

Below: In 1907 auto-train working received a brief try-out. Two Sharps 2-4-0 tender engines were rebuilt as tanks and two six-wheeled coaches were cut about and remounted on a bogie-frame to form a trailer. *Cambrian Official.*

Above: Jubilation – the crowd and principal participants in the opening ceremony of the new extension and terminal station at Pwllheli, 19 July 1907. The old main station building was re-built stone by stone at Aberdovey. *The National Library of Wales.*

Below and right: In March 1908 five more 'Jones Goods' were received, this time built by Beyer Peacock & Co. They were curiously numbered 15, 31, 38, 42 and 54, and while No 38 remained unmoved the others were equally curiously re-numbered 99-102 just to boost the Cambrian locomotive numberings into three figures. The Beyer engines had even better cabs than their predecessors; they came right over the footplate on pillars. No 102, the highest number in the Cambrian stock register, is manned by Driver Tom Caffrey on 4 July, 1913. Here is No 101 on Sawmill Siding, Aberdovey. Note the creosote tank for sleepers. *H. W. Burman.*

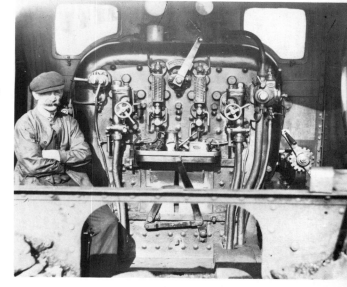

Above left: Before No 31 had time to be renumbered 100, she shot off the rails on 7 August 1908 in the dip at Nantmawr Junction and towed a horse-box and a Great Central Railways brake-third between the Llanfyllin line and the Ballast Siding, thereby providing the locals with something nearly as exciting to watch as a travelling circus. The driver got the blame and the sack. Maybe the fact that the train was a private charter job moving a director's household goods and farm stock did not help! *Cambrian Official.*

Below left: Dinas Mawddwy, c 1912, with 2-4-0 No 28. *G. M. Perkins.*

Above: The last pair of Jones corridor coaches were built in 1908 and were locker tricomposites with a diminutive portion at the end for a guard. They were rebuilt as refreshment serveries and became known as the 'Tea Cars'. Many people remember the long struggle down the narrow corridors, climbing over suitcases and squeezing past people to reach and edge their way, elbows tucked in, round the little buffet space – and the perilous return journey. As might have been expected, the buffets were staffed by Spiers & Ponds. *Cambrian Official.*

Below: In 1908, as part of an economy drive brought about by rising wages, the work in the paintshop was cut by introducing an overall bronze-green carriage livery, relieved by single middle chrome yellow lining. This is Builth Road Station in 1902, with a 2-4-0 on a down train waiting to cross an up train. *G. M. Perkins.*

Above: In 1910 No 21 was the first of the 'Small Sharps' to be re-built with a higher boiler pressure and the shorter Jones chimney; she lost none of her good appearance in the process. She is seen at Aberdovey on 24 September 1912, on the 9.20 up Coast train. *H. W. Burman.*

Below: Afon Wen about 1910. The marked similarity in appearance between the Cambrian rebuilds of the old 2-4-0s and the Webb engines of the London & North Western is exemplified here in Cambrian 2-4-0 No 29 and an unidentified 0-6-2 'Coal Tank'. *Courtesy of Ifor Higgon.*

Top right: On Saturday 29 July 1911, with the aid of a Light Railway Order, a Treasury grant, and a handsome subscription from David (later first Lord) Davies, the MP for Montgomeryshire, the Cambrian re-opened the Mawddwy Railway after an extensive re-construction. Dinas Mawddwy station is here decorated for the occasion. *Courtesy of W. E Hayward.*

Centre right: The completed new Barmouth Bridge, c 1910. *J. Valentine.*

Bottom right: The surviver from the Van Railway at Caersws about 1910. *Courtesy of Evan Howells.*

Right: From 1867 the Cambrian had given connecting passenger and goods facilities adjacent to its station at Cemmes Road to the Mawddwy Railway, until the latter's near physical and financial collapse, which went agonisingly on from 1903 to 1908. In re-opening the Mawddwy, the Cambrian took on yet another old Manning Wardle – by now the oldest, Works No 140 of 1864. Named *Mawddwy*, it was rebuilt before going back into service in 1911 and becoming Cambrian No 30. A similar but heavier workmate, *Disraeli*, was scrapped at the takeover. *L&GRP.*

Centre right: Nevertheless *Disraeli*, via 'her' or 'his' salvaged cylinder block and crank-axle, did good service for many years after the official scrapping date as the works air-compressor. Note the multi-rope drive – a remedy for the 1914-18 wartime shortage of leather? *E. Colclough.*

Below: Decorations for the Royal occasion – Aberystwyth ready for the arrival of King George V and Queen Mary on 15 July 1911, when 'His Majesty the King placed the foundation stone at the north-west angle of the main front of the Great Hall and Her Majesty the Queen placed a corresponding stone on the south-east angle of the same building' – so reads the Report of the Council for The National Library of Wales. *National Library of Wales.*

Far right above: A 'Jones Goods' 0-6-0 arriving at Aberdovey on an up goods in early summer, 1911. *H. W. Burman.*

Far right below: A 'Sharps Goods' 0-6-0 on a southbound local passenger train leaving Harlech, 8 July 1911. *H. W. Burman.*

Above: 'Aston Goods' No 79 on a down Coast goods– two Cambrian vans followed by low two-plank slate wagons – approaching Harlech, 24 July 1911. *H. W. Burman.*

Left: In 1912 the section of line between Newtown and Moat Lane was doubled. The principal feature created through this requirement was the Doughty Bridge across the Severn. *C. C. Green.*

Below Left: Three generations of Stationmasters. Mr Fryer, seen here posed at Abermule with the tablet (marked Abermule and Montgomery, which would authorise the train to go ahead in safety) was the grandfather of the small boy in the photograph on page 22. Later his own son became stationmaster at Abermule. The tablet-controlling instruments were in the low building behind the engine and not in a signalbox. Knowing the Fryers' reputations for the careful working of their stations one can surely say that had the second Mr. Fryer not been on holiday, there would not have been the accident there in 1921, despite the odd arrangement. *Courtesy of W. R. Fryer.*

Above: 'Sharps Goods' No 14 waits at the head of Aberdovey Harbour Branch on 16 July 1912, until the through train signalled on the main line has passed. Note that she is propelling one wagon and will have a short train behind the tender. It was quite normal procedure on the Cambrian to propel or to propel and pull simultaneously in order to work awkwardly placed sidings. *H. W. Burman.*

Below: The extremely popular Vale of Rheidol Light Railway with a gauge of 1 ft 11½ in had been operating from its own terminus near Aberystwyth station since 1902 and had a mixed-gauge exchange siding with the Cambrian near Llanbadarn. It was absorbed into the Cambrian system on 1 August 1913 – the last of a numerous series of takeovers, which brought the total mileage to 241 owned, plus 57 miles worked for subsidiary companies. *Lewis The Mart – A. J. Lewis.*

Above: Much ado about nothing: Sharps 2-4-0 No 53 makes a tremendous pother about taking a turn on the trailer car local on 4 July 1913, leaving Aberdovey. *H. W. Burman.*

Above left: Besides the little Bagnall seen on the previous page (known affectionately by the valley folk as 'Coffee Pot'), the Cambrian took over with the Vale of Rheidol two 2-6-2 tank engines, the only ones ever to have been built by Davies & Metcalfe. As the firm had no experience of designing entire steam locomotives they appealed for help to the Lynton & Barnstaple and received a set of drawings for a narrow-gauge 2-6-2 tank. *W. L. Good.*

Centre left: 'Sharps Goods' No 39 on an up goods appraching Lwyngwril, 9 July 1914. Note the use of lowsided wagons, all two-plank, even for casks as in the one behind the van. *H. W. Burman*

Below left: 'Aston Goods' No 87 approaching Aberdovey station in 1913. The Harbour Branch leading to Sands Sidings and Port Aberdovey is on the right. *H. W. Burman.*

Right: Dignity – The Ticket Inspectors. The summer-relieving inspector at the back wears a uniform hat only. *Courtesy of H. S. Humphries.*

1914 – 1922:
The War Years and Finale

The Great War has been de-personalised to mere numbers as the 1914-18 war, and now even further down to World War I to distinguish it from World War II. It was reality to those who lived through it and the four years of neglect it entailed for the Cambrian (and all the other small railways) brought about decline to a point beyond recovery. It revived for the Cambrian very briefly some of the failed mineral workings and created a temporary demand for home-grown timber, mainly for pitprops. But when it was over most of this indigenous freight traffic had gone for all time.

Above left: 'Small Sharps' No 16 near Aberdovey, c 1915. *H. W. Burman.*

Above: 'Large Sharps' No 86 on a north-bound train late one evening in 1915 between Harlech and Pensarn. *H. W. Burman.*

Left: There was wartime shortage of engines because several were working the South-to-North 'Jellicoe Specials' on part of the route between the South Wales coalfields and Scapa Flow and others were working out to Shrewsbury, Crewe, and even over to the North Midlands. This prompted the rebuild by Beyer Peacock in 1915 of No 34, one of the ex-Metropolitan 4-4-0 tanks. No 36 was converted at Oswestry in 1916 at less cost. The lighter axle-weight so obtained enabled them to be used more widely, but they were never a success. The tenders came from 'Sharps Goods' 0-6-0s. *Cambrian Official.*

Below left: Despite the war there was still holiday traffic on the coast and 1915 and 1916 saw the conversion of two older six-wheeled coaches into observation cars with reversible tram-type seating, for use on the Coast route. *G. H. W. Clifford.*

Below: From 1915 onwards, repainted engines appeared in a new livery of broad French grey edged signal red, with the word 'CAMBRIAN' in middle chrome yellow on the tender. 'CAMBRIAN' was also tried out in French grey. The stumpier, built-up Jones chimney replaced the more stylish Aston design. No 79 is at Sands Siding Aberdovey on 12 July 1915. It is not clear whether the change back, not to the old blue-grey but to the 'pinky' French grey, was inspired by a leaning towards the 'Entente Cordiale' with our allies across the Channel, but it would accord with the sentimentality of the time. *H. W. Burman.*

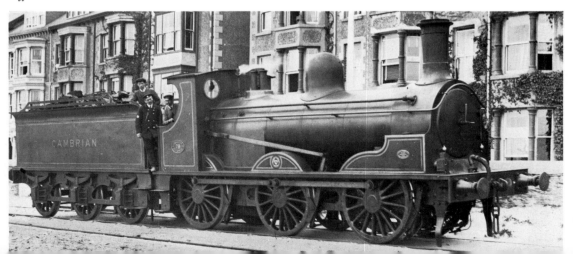

Above: 'Aston Goods' 0-6-0 on passenger duty leaving Aberdovey on 3 August 1918. The train includes one through runner – a GWR coach. *H. W. Burman.*

Left: 'Aston Goods' No 88 leaving Llanbedr for Dyffryn Ardudwy c 1916. *H. W. Burman.*

Above right: No 86 leaving Caersws on a short local train to Whitchurch. The cast-iron notices were painted in white letters on a green background, being the same green (approximating BR parcels road-van green) as was used with white and sometimes a lighter green on the stations. *Collection C. C. Green.*

Right: Barmouth Junction East Box, 1918, with a GWR through train via Dolgelley exchanging tablets. *H. W. Burman.*

Below right: Machynlleth about 1919. 'Large Sharps' No 66 with a Great Western through train via Buttington Junction for Aberystwyth. *H. W. Burman.*

Below: 'Small Sharps' No 50 racing along the estuary wall towards Aberdovey c 1918. *H. W. Burman.*

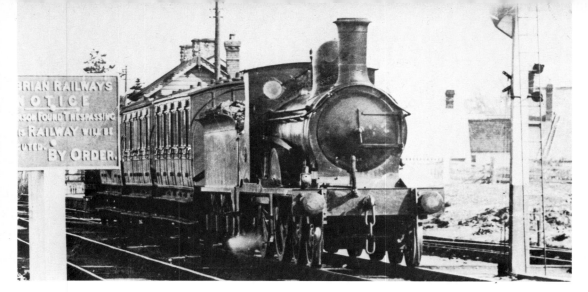

Right: The Cambrian accomplishes the impossible – two wagons interlocked and both suspended in mid-air. Towyn? *Chief Civil Engineer's Office, NE Region.*

Below: 'Sharps Goods' No 14 entering Machynlleth station in 1919. It is not known whether the running figure wishes to impart some information or wants a lift. *H. W. Burman.*

Bottom: Sharps 2-4-0 No 41 on a Coast local approaching Copper Hill Street Bridge and Craig y Don (No 4) tunnel, Aberdovey, 23 July 1919. *H. W. Burman.*

Left: The period after the Great War was naturally unsettled. Railway revenues could not pay for wages comparable with what the munition workers had been getting and wages restrictions and staff cut-backs led to strikes. So passengers were handling their own luggage in September 1919. Those enormous hats *had* to be worn on the journeys – they simply could not be packed. *A. J. Lewis.*

Below: When the Cambrian trains ceased to run altogether many people 'escaped' from Aberystwyth via the Great Western down the Manchester & Milford route to South Wales. *A. J. Lewis.*

Left: While the original caption to this picture was 'Attempt to stop Great Western Motor Bus at Aberystwyth', the unconcerned manner of the gentleman reading his newspaper with his feet on the mudguard of the bus belies the alleged seriousness of the affair. *A. J. Lewis.*

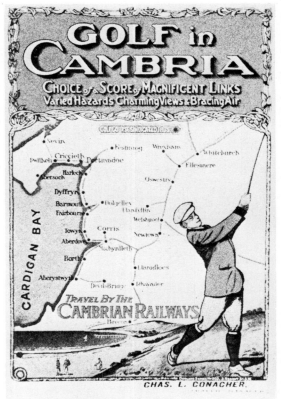

CAMBRIA'S CALL TO GOLFERS.

Right and above: Advertising comparisons – Connacher's golfer of 1910 and Williamson's of around 1920 with his bathing belle. *M. E. M. Lloyd and H. R. Thornton.*

Below: Aberystwyth Station c 1920. In this year on this station at the age of four, the author was spellbound by an engine with big bulgy sloping cylinders, a polished brass dome and an enormous chimney. The following year at Builth Wells, where the boarding house was next to the line, cemented a life-long alliance with dignified shiny black engines with red oval number plates, and the resounding word 'CAMBRIAN' on their tenders. *A. J. Lewis.*

Above: Staff at Aberystwyth about 1920 (strange that a goods train should have been backed right down into a passenger terminus: and one feels that the photographer might have got the wheel-tapper not to hold his hammer as if it was sticking up out of the stationmaster's hat). With the many excursions (including, of course, those to the 1916 National Eisteddfodd), the only carriage liveries these gentlemen are not on record as having seen in their own station were those of the North British and of the Glasgow & South Western. Today's Cambrian modeller is thus free to tell his friends 'Bring your own stock'. *Collection C. C. Green.*

Below: Few photographers caught Cambrian engines 'going foreign', but here is 'Aston Goods' No 74 on a through-running train from South Wales at Merthyr Tydfil. The angle of taking recalls admirably the knack these small engines had of hiding behind their tenders. *H. L. Hopwood: now in Loco Club of Gt. Britain's K. Nunn Collection.*

Above: 'Small Sharps' No 50 on an up Coast train made up entirely of six-wheelers, c 1920. *G. H. W. Clifford.*

Below: 4-4-0 No 36, once the Metropolitan Underground tank engine *Aurora*, at Aberdovey in 1920. *G. H. W. Clifford.*

Above right: One of the last batch of 'Jones Goods' was derailed in Talerddig Cutting, when a landslide (one of many over the years) derailed two engines in 1921. There were no direct services for two days. No 54 is seen on January 19, 1921, the day after the accident. Much worse was to follow. *Edwards Bros. Newtown.*

Right: Abermule, 26 January 1921 – the Cambrian's third 'classic' accident, when the fireman of No 82, a 'Large Sharps', took back from a young porter-signalman the tablet referring to Montgomery – Abermule which he had just traversed. So the train left Abermule heading straight for an express, which had already left Newtown along the single track. After ringing Abermule to see if the express had cleared the section, the station staff at Newtown stood about

in stunned silence. 'We knew what was going to happen; we were waiting to be told where it had happened', they said. *E. Colclough.*

Below right: Abermule, 26 January 1921. Under one coach, four bogies of two different companies. The fireman of No 95 came to his senses walking about down the line from the wreckage and clutching the tablets from both engines. He never recalled the details of his search after instinctively snatching his own tablet before jumping from his engine. The crew of No 82 were both killed, along with the Company Chairman, Lord Herbert Vane-Tempest, and 16 other passengers. The crew of No 95 did go back to driving, but 'kept seeing things coming at them round curves', their mates said. *Edward Bros. Newtown.*

Above: As a hasty stop-gap replacement for Nos 82 and 95, two elderly ex-Great Western engines were bought from the Bute Docks Supply Co. Originally Beyer Peacock 'singles', they had been converted to 2-4-0s. No 10, ex-GW, No 213, is seen at Harlech in 1922. The other was No 1, ex-GWR No 212. *H. W. Burman.*

Below: By contrast with the disaster of January 1921, the Cambrian's association with the greatest influence upon communication and thought the world has ever known slipped by unnoticed. On 15 August 1921 a graceful steam yacht entered the Dovey estuary and was moored at the old quay. The relevent entry in the Cambrian Railways – Port of Aberdovey register reads: *Name and Description of Vessel –*

Yacht *Elettra ; Merchant's Name –* Marconi. The charge was £2.21. That evening the folk of Aberdovey gathered on the quayside wonderstruck to hear organ music broadcast from Waunfawr 40 miles away. Could words and music really climb above Cefn ddu, cross mountains and water, and come steeply down over Fridd cefn isaf to sea level? But by the end of 1922 we had heard '2MT Writtle calling!' Soon after families and friends were gathering each evening around enormous contraptions of valves and coils which served up to six sets of headphones to listen to 2LO London, 5IT Birmingham, and the other early BBC stations. *Photochrom.*

Above: No 77 taking water at Llwngwril in 1921. The diminutive water-tower was at the north end of the up platform; it fed also a water-column at the south end, which was kept from freezing by a built-in coal stove. *H. W. Burman.*

Right: 'Aston Goods' No 78 on a northbound goods train passing the up starter signal of Llwyngwril in 1921. The white disc and the ruby-gold danger glass are still there, but green supplanted white for 'all clear' during the war. *H. W. Burman.*

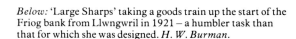

Below: 'Large Sharps' taking a goods train up the start of the Friog bank from Llwngwril in 1921 – a humbler task than that for which she was designed. *H. W. Burman.*

Above: A Vale of Rheidol train bound for Devils Bridge crossing 'The Black Bridge' in 1921. *W. L. Good.*

Below: Before leaving in 1918 Herbert Jones ordered the Cambrian's last new engines, a further five of his 0-6-0 Goods, from Beyer Peacock & Co, this time all numbered to fill in gaps left from scrappings. Nos 15, 29, 31, 42 and 54 were delivered during 1918 and 1919. No 31 heads an up Coast train south of Harlech in 1921. *H. W. Burman.*

Above right and right: Although the Railways Act 1921, which prescribed the legal and financial framework of the absorption of the small Welsh railway lines into the Great Western system, did not become effective until 1 January 1922, the Great Western took a fatherly interest in their affairs in advance. In the case of the Cambrian the GWR 'lent' them two former broad-gauge 0-4-4 tank engines then running as 4-4-0 tender engines, Nos 3521 and 3546 (seen here at Aberystwyth in 1925), as from August 1921. But useful as she may have been on a short-term basis, No 3521 cannot have been in the best of health when first she steamed over the border; she was back at Swindon for overhaul in 1923. As a loan, these two engines were not a generous one. Actually the book transaction which recorded their transfer noted 'sale'; in the financial climate of 1921 the Great Western gave away nothing. *A. W. Croughton.*

Below right: A valedictory – the management of the Cambrian assembled for a parting photograph on 25 March 1922. G. C. Macdonald (Engineer & Locomotive Superintendent) and S. Williamson (Secretary and General Manager), each dutifully and economically filling two posts, are seated third and fourth from the left. *The Story of the Cambrian.*

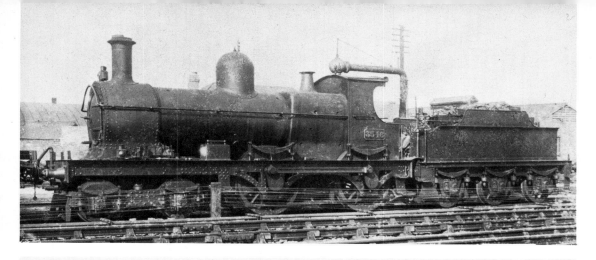

OL-YSGRIF

A dyna'r hen Gambrian. O'i chymharu â chw-mniau eraill, menter fechan ydoedd. Yr oedd prynu dwy injan newydd yn gymaint ymgymeriad iddi ag ydoedd adeiladu deugain i'r London and North Western. Ni fu ei stoc o beiriannau erioed yn fwy na chant, a phrin y cyrhaeddodd y trac dri chan milltir o hyd. Yr oedd llai nag un cerbyd y filltir o drac ar gyfer cario teithwyr a saith wagen y filltir yn unig ar gyfer cludo nwyddau yn lleol yn ogystal ag o fewn cylch ehangach.

Os ydyw ysbryd anturiaeth yn cyfrif o gwbl, yr oedd hon yn fenter fawr, a thrist yw meddwl fod y Ddraig Cymru, Rosyn Coch Lancaster, a phlu Tywysgog Cymru bellach wedi eu dileu.

Postcript

That was the old Cambrian. In comparison with other companies it was a small affair. The buying of two new engines was as large an undertaking as it was for the London & North Western to build 40 or more: and its stock of engines never quite reached the hundred mark. Track mileage barely attained even 300 and its passenger traffic was catered for with less than one carriage per mile of track. Only seven wagons per mile conveyed all its local and outwards goods.

If spirit counts, then it was a great affair. And the painting over of the Dragon of Wales, the Red Rose of Lancaster, and the Prince of Wales' Feathers was something to be regretted.

The Cambrian under the GWR 1922-1947

The Barmouth Road

The Great Western had planned that, by backing the promotion of a chain of little railways, the Vale of Llangollen, the Llangollen & Corwen, the Denbigh, Ruthin & Corwen, the Corwen & Bala and the Bala & Dolgelley they would reach the coast and compete with the London & North-Western's ambitions via Carnarvon and Afon Wen. The Aberystwyth & Welsh Coast defeated them by getting its Dolgelley Branch opened to Penmaenpool by 3 July 1865 more than three years before the first train from Bala coasted into Dolgelley. At first all the Great Western's too-heavy engines had to be taken off and turned at Dolgelley; but during the 1920s the branch was upgraded first to GWR Yellow category and then to blue for the Moguls and the 'Manors' followed later still. So 'The Barmouth Road' became a major alternative to 'The Aber Road'.

Below: With both safety valves blowing 4-4-0 'Dukedog' No 9014 pilots No 3210 gently round the Berwyn curve above the strikingly beautiful gorge of the Dee. 9.10 Paddington to Pwllheli. *Ifor Higgon*

Right: 'Catch them slow and working Hard'. 0-6-0 Collett Goods Nos 2214 and 2204 at full blast ten feet from the top of the 1 in 94 climb over Garneddwen summit. Pwllheli to Blackpool excursion. *Ifor Higgon*

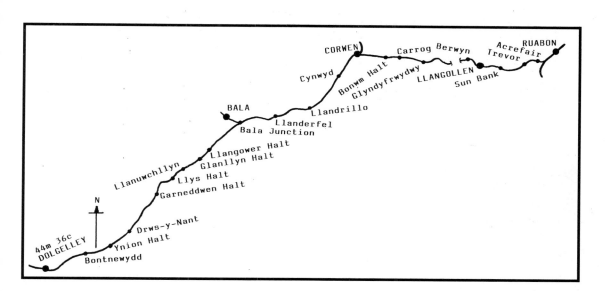

Above: No 4386 o f the 2-6-0 Mogul or 'Shortened Prairie' class, watched by the signalman, coasts gently away from Drws-y-nant as the fireman readies himself to take the train staff. 11am Saturdays Only Ruabon to Pwllheli, 11 September 1937. *Ifor Higgon*

Below: 0-6-0 pannier tank No 1763 of 1892 pilots 4-4-0 'Bulldog' No 3359 *Tregeagle* out of Bontnewydd taking the nine-coach 1.15 Barmouth to Chester up to Garneddwen. 25 August 1934. *Ifor Higgon*

Introduction

The Government had plans to nationalise all railways by retaining full control after the 1914-18 war. However the Civil Service advisors pointed out that while freight charges had been pegged at 1913 rates when operating costs were 63% of receipts; operating costs had risen by 1921 to 115% of receipts. Besides this materials only had been paid for and not labour and works costs for the millions of pounds worth of munitions made in railway works. War payments for use of railways had been fixed at only the sums necessary to maintain dividends at the 1913 figures, and a mere £60million had been voted for distribution as reparation for arrears of maintenance and war damage.

At that time a nationalised industry run at a legally enforced loss was inconceivable and the wreckage was handed back to the unfortunate shareholders.

Most of the independent companies had applied the annual payments in maintenance of dividends right up to 1921 and were in sore straits through lack of maintenance. In default of fair treatment from the nation, amalgamation was the only solution and as from the vesting day 1 January 1922 the holders of Cambrian Ordinary Capital No 1 shares and of Coast Ordinary Consolidated Stock found themselves left with only £2.86 for every £100 they or their parents had held after the Connacher shake-up of the 1890s. (*Cambrian Railways Album* p40).

All this was quickly swept under the carpet by the press and most writers got down to forecasting and discovering with delight the advantages of amalgamation to the railway user, to the country as a whole, and perhaps even to the railwayman. Management did not lag behind and the Chairman of the Great Western, Lord Mildmay of Flete, pronounced 'amalgamation has resulted in a better service for the public and the better working of the railways from every point of view'.

Against this background the irrepressible liveliness of the railwaymen of Wales soon made itself felt and in September 1923 the *Great Western Magazine* carried an article which proclaimed that a prominent railwayman had wittily remarked that 'The Cambrian had taken over the Great Western'. Even further, in 1926, the railway choral societies combined to hold an Eisteddfodd, at Swindon!

Starting with a good welcome to 'the army of fresh colleagues' from the General Manager the Great Western did do its best to treat all fairly and with amazing rapidity the men from the Cambrian and from the South Wales companies gained promotion all over the new larger system. As one old friend put it with a twinkle in his eye 'Well, once they'd got the best they had to use it hadn't they?'

Initially the newly-appointed General Manager, Felix Pole, saw this as a problem rather than an asset in higher management circles; how to dispose of so many officers each used to directing his own little show? and he had to have an argument which would appeal to and convince his Board of Directors. Accordingly he reported that many of them were not sufficiently proficient or up to date to be retained in modernised railway management and that it would be more efficient and cheaper in the long run to award pensions or golden handshakes to make the way clear for the younger and more active men.

And so the old hierarchies went at a single blow, mostly on less than generous terms, but to many of them the thought of giving up their established ways of independence and of changing to the service of distant masters was enough to make them wish to go. The boards of directors had all been dismissed by legislation, only the Cambrian and a few others were considered important enough to rate a director on the Great Western board to represent his area.

On 24 March 1922 the Cambrian issued its last weekly notice and the Great Western assumed practical control of 'The Cambrian Division' as it was first termed. Soon the mistake was realised and by July the name of individuality had been expunged from the record; henceforth it would be 'The Central Wales Division'!

As another gentleman put it 'the era of pinstripes, spats and bowler hats had begun'.

AUTHOR'S NOTE

As in *Cambrian Railways Album* to which this book is a sequel place names are referred to and spelt as they were then. October 1924 was a landmark in the fostering of amateur interest in railways; the Stephenson Locomotive Society published its first journal.

Always a trendsetter the Great Western readily acceded to requests for private or organised visits to sheds and works, all they asked was a donation of one shilling to the Railwaymen's Benevolent Association by each visitor. Photography was freely allowed and thus when assembling a book about this period picture research becomes more a matter of selection for story and interest rather than a hunt for the rare and elusive few.

The publicity department was well-run and the neat little booklets aimed at the railway enthusiast in the 1920s showed that the staff were well aware of the value of 'catching them young'. Unfortunately at that time the author had no camera and not too many shillings, but many contented hours were spent on railway bridges in the formation of a worthy coating of grime on forearms and chin, and less domestically acceptable, on shirts.

Where a photograph used has borne no discoverable name it has been credited to 'Anon'. I feel that 'Collection C. C. Green' is out of place for the more recent photographs, and I trust then that no one will be offended. If a photographer does see his work so credited in this book may I quote the old foreman to the old driver whose engine had been worked by another while he was not on duty 'it was an important turn and we had to have the best engine'.

A 'Farewell to the Cambrian' group taken in 1921. The station-master is the same Mr W. T. Fryer who appears on the left in the Llanbrynmair photograph on page 22. Taken at Caersws while No 35, a Chapman & Furneaux 0-6-0T, was working the Van Branch. *Courtesy of W. R. Fryer*

Soon to Vanish

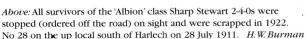

Above: All survivors of the 'Albion' class Sharp Stewart 2-4-0s were stopped (ordered off the road) on sight and were scrapped in 1922. No 28 on the up local south of Harlech on 28 July 1911. *H. W. Burman*

Above right: Three of the six invaluable Nasmyth Wilson 0-4-4Ts went in the 1922 Swindon scrapping blunder. No 3, seen here, and No 8 survived until October 1922. The 9.18 down local north of Aberdovey, 10 July 1914. *H. W. Burman*

Right: The four ex-Metropolitan 4-4-0Ts and the two tender rebuilds were all out of service by June 1923. No 37 at Barmouth c1920. This negative is underexposed and had to be bleached out and converted to a red image so that the blue sensitive printing paper would react as if it had been better exposed. Also the film had buckled a fraction and lost definition on the right. *G. H. W. Clifford*

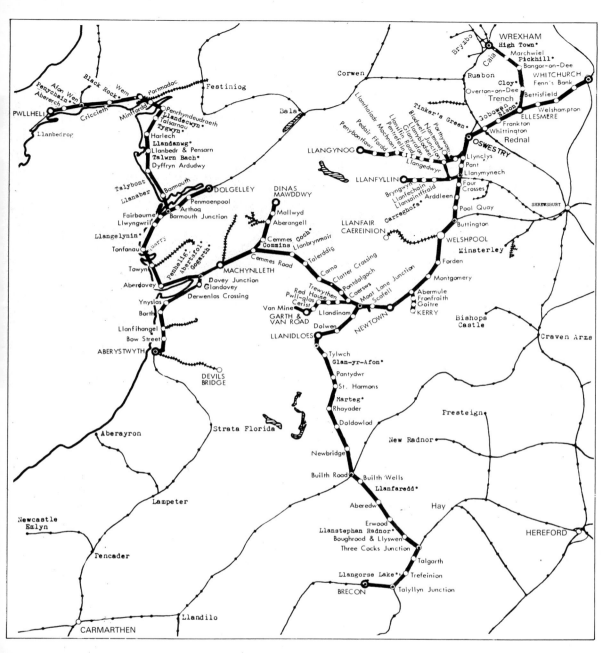

The Great Western's Cambrian

This map shows all the Cambrian lines operated at any time during the period covered by the book; the only closures made by the Great Western being those of the short link between Nantmawr Junction and Blodwell Junction and of the relatively small Van branch.

All the new halts added by the Great Western are distinguished by the addition of an asterisk* and the precise placing of these within the limited spaces has not been attempted.

Bus services are not shown; the GWR direct running of buses was transferred to the area companies by the 1930s but the company's faith in its capacity to remain for all time the provider of transport for its areas was evidenced by the running of a bus service between Aberystwyth and Machynlleth via Talybont in direct competition with its own trains along the coast.

Above: The Men of the Past. Directors and Officers of the old Cambrian on a farewell visit to Aberystwyth in May 1922. Lt-Col David Davies MP (third from right) stayed on as Great Western director representing Cambrian interests and Mr H. Warwick (fifth from right) became District Traffic Manager, and one or two others stayed on for a while. *The Story of the Cambrian*

Below: The Men of the Future. The Premium Apprentices of 1919 and 1920, F. S. Roberts (back row, right) stayed at Oswestry all his life and rose to be the last Works Manager. J. Colclough (front row, centre) attained a position of responsibility at Swindon, the remainder fared well in other spheres and Chetma Bharsa (second from left, back row) returned to Bombay. *J. Maclardy*

Above: The Oswestry Works Management. Some retired and some stayed on. The Works Manager himself (front row fourth from left) Mr E. Colclough stayed in command under the new regime and became the Divisional Superintendent. Mr F. S. Roberts (back row, fourth from left) is now the Draughtsman. *Courtesy of F. S. Roberts*

Right: The keynote of the last Weekly Notice was still expiation for the Abermule disaster of the year before. *Courtesy of J. Spoonley*

Below: This cartoon bears a joke within the joke. Gwr, which is pronounced a little like goo rr (but only by the English) is the Welsh term for man, husband, or more properly 'the head of the house'. Now it was to be borne on the uniform caps of unmarried youths and striplings and the folk in the Central Wales Division were quick to see the joke. *The South Wales News*

A SURVIVAL OF TITLE.

DICK GERMAN

THE GREAT WESTERN: "Hooray! Never even blew me cap off!"

"None of the companies which survive the amalgamation upheaval have come out of it with so much enhanced prestige as the Great Western. It is the only one to retain its old and familiar title."—"South Wales News" leading article.

Reproduced from the "South Wales News" Monday, November 27, 1922.

1922-1927
Old Stock and New Management

The first thoughts were seemingly focused on 'how safe were the Welsh engines?' Swindon-directed staff worked overtime on inspections. In those days 'stopped' was stopped literally whenever and wherever and the engine, coach, or wagon was immediately dragged off to Swindon Works. Thus the works had no control over the rate of arrival and there was only one standard of repair — 100% overhaul. By the Autumn of 1922, 148 of the 800 odd Welsh company engines were at Swindon alongside 192 Great Western engines, making 340 in all.

The situation was an impossible one, engines lay outside all around, frames were stacked sometimes three high inside and drastic and positive action was needed. Someone then asked what would today be called 'the sixty four thousand dollar question'. 'Are all services being maintained without these engines? — and if the answer is "Yes" should we not cut them all up?' The answer was 'Yes' and they were all cut up — perhaps not quite all for someone at Oswestry wisely had been keeping an ear to the rails and a very strong case was made for retaining the lighter small engines for the branches and for which the smallest Great Western engines would have been too heavy. Otherwise they were scrapped even if they had been re-boilered within the previous five years.

Subsequently the Accountant's Department raised a few awkward questions (it has been said) for there were some sizeable bills still outstanding for parts and materials from the last Cambrian repairs to engines that had thus been scrapped, and the Great Western had to pay them. Mr C. B. Collett the newly-appointed Chief Mechanical Engineer was not in the least perturbed; he was not known to have actually written that to make omelettes one has to

break eggs, but it would have been quite in keeping with his style and manner to have done so.

It is now worth pausing for a while to look at the simple system the Great Western had for the designation of routes and of the engines allowed over them for this was not a matter of haphazard rostering. Bridges, curves and track construction and condition are all limiting factors to the length and weight of engines which can be despatched with safety along any particular route. The system of classification divided the power or pull of the engines into six groups from E down to A with Ungrouped for the minor lightweights at the bottom of the scale. These six were designated again by reference to the heaviest axleweight (usually that of the driving axle) that an engine could impose upon the track when fully topped up with water and coal; and here there were four classifications for which colours were used to distinguish the one from the other. No engine having an axleweight exceeding 14 tons was allowed along an Uncoloured route, and an Uncoloured engine could literally go anywhere except certain private sidings. Engines of up to 16 tons heaviest axleweight were allowed on Yellow routes and above but not on Uncoloured routes. Blue routes could take up to 17 tons 12cwt and over Red routes the heaviest express engines could be driven, but these elite machines were permitted nowhere else. On the engines themselves the route colour was indicated by a small disc of colour painted on the cab side, and within the disc was the power letter.

So the 'Saints' and 'Stars' flaunted Red Cs and Ds and the 'Flowers' and the 'Cities' had to be content with Red As which restricted where they could go and showed that they could not pull much of a train either. The serene and super-powerful 28xx class 2-8-0s went their less restricted way as Blue Es. There were a number of very efficient types in the Blue category ranging from B up to D but of all this mighty fleet of Blue and Red engines none was of the slightest use over the Cambrian for its main lines were of only Yellow standard and its branches were more Uncoloured than Uncoloured, ie they were even more lightly constructed.

Left: A rare old assortment of motive power. On the left is a Great Western 2-4-0 Barnum, facing an ex-Cambrian Jones Goods. On the right outside is a Great Western 0-6-0PT buffered from behind by ex-Cambrian No 30 as GW No 824, the old ex-Mawddwy Railway 0-6-0ST from Manning Wardle. Nearer in line is ex-Cambrian No 12 as GW No 1130 originally the Metropolitan Railways 4-4-0 condensing tank No 11 Latona. Clearest of all is ex-Cambrian No 26 as GW No 820, a Chapman & Furneaux 0-6-0T once on the Lambourn Valley Light Railway. A bit of another Barnum completes the picture. *A. W. Croughton*

Above: The obvious choice for goods work was William Dean's 0-6-0 2301 class built between 1883 and 1899. This one can be rightly called 'The Unknown Soldier'. Just back from Salonika, and the end-of-war shortage of brass has precluded the re-casting of a new number plate. Photographed at Penmaenpool in 1922. *J. P. Richards*

Above: Goods engines they may have been by design and intention but in the Cambrian area they were to be invaluable as passenger engines. Note the smartly re-liveried Cambrian coach. At Barmouth Junction c1924. *H. W. Burman*

Left: The small-wheeled Stellas built in 1885 handled short trains very well indeed, smart acceleration and a fairish gradient climbing capacity were their characteristics as long as they were not overloaded. No 3519 at Machynlleth c1923. Note the 2,500 gallon tender. *J. P. Richards*

Below: The Barnums, William Dean's best 2-4-0 design built in 1889, were very popular with their crews and they lasted in Central Wales for a longer time than the other small passenger types. No 3213 is on the old Cambrian turntable at Machynlleth c1923. *J. P. Richards*

Right: Several of the 3232 class of express engines built in 1892/93 worked in the area and the last two survivors of the class ended their days at Oswestry. Their 6ft 7in driving wheels were the largest diameter ever to work over the Central Wales Division. Seen at Machynlleth c1923. *J. P. Richards*

Thus the only engines which could be drafted on to the Cambrian were the 4-4-0 'Duke' class, the 0-6-0 Dean Goods and a handful of older Dean engines in various states of build or rebuild. Sir John Betjeman has written: 'The only good things to come out of the Victorian era were the Great Western engines. They were wholly satisfying, wholly efficient and wholly beautiful.' The Central Wales Division became the place to go and see them enjoying a long Indian summer of loving care and pride of place.

Carriages and wagons too received the benefit of summary jurisdiction and many obsolete timber-framed specimens went on sight, particularly wagons because the accidental inclusion of an elderly example at the head of the longer train which the Great Western sought to introduce resulted in its being torn apart in a jerky start on a gradient.

Station layout and signalling too came under scrutiny and the *Great Western Magazine* became full of paragraphs about places being improved, brought up to date, modernised and even brought up to Great Western standards. At 13 stations the tablet instruments were still in the booking offices.

The first time a 'Duke' No 3271 *Eddystone* appeared on the coast it was taking a military special to Portmadoc, and the crew had to return tender-first all the way to Barmouth Junction to turn on the triangle and then continue backwards to rejoin the train at Portmadoc. For a company which applied main line standards to every branch line this sort of carry-on would not do. Even turntables would have to be reviewed as soon as possible. It was further proposed that the Coast line should be extended to Nevin with a branch to Abersoch, old Cambrian ambitions revived, but as before nothing

came of the proposal. More practicable was the continuance of the original Cambrian policy of doubling track between Welshpool and Dovey Junction wherever possible and several additional portions were so treated to the great benefit of summer working. The civil engineering staff were in for some years of feverish activity.

Inside the works at Swindon repairs would proceed at matching pace for, whatever the overall financial position, the Repairs and Renewals Fund had been kept up. Modified Dean Goods boilers were designed for fitting to many of the Cambrian's Aston and Jones Goods engines and which also fitted many South Wales engines. To ease the strain on the Boiler Shop many of these No 9 boilers were made outside by Kitsons, by the Vulcan Foundry, and by the Yorkshire Engine Co.

On the administrative side the general policy was 'The Great Western does everything' and Spiers and Pond's lost their refreshment rooms and luncheon baskets franchise.

It was a tremendous challenge and the new allies turned to and met it with a will. Mind you there were a few hitches initially, such as when the first of the 10 o'clock Friday night excursions from Paddington started. Drawn usually by Barnums the trippers could expect to be sitting on Aberystwyth beach by 6 o'clock on the Saturday morning; unless the train was halted at a lonely signalbox whistling into the night and trying to draw the attention of the next signalman on to get him back from the river to accept the forgotten extra. It fell to a solitary Welsh pheasant to essay a token objection. It flew headlong on to the front vacuum pipe of a Great Western engine approaching Welshpool, knocked it off the stopper, and brought the train to a summary halt.

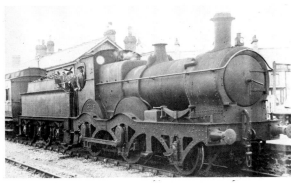

Left: A few of the Barnums (so called because the type was often rostered to draw the Barnum and Bailey Circus Specials) had been modernised with domeless belpaire boilers with top feed. No 3224 at Towyn in 1922. *H. W. Burman*

Below: At first there were not very many 'Dukes' actually shedded in the area; they were barely 25 years old and they could not yet be spared from other work. No 3270 *Earl of Devon* at Machynlleth c1923. *J. P. Richards*

Bottom: The 3521 class of 4-4-0 had been converted from an unstable design of 0-4-4T some of which had been built for the broad gauge. No 3546 seen here at Machynlleth in 1923 was one of the pair sold to the Cambrian in 1921 after the Abermule smash. *J. P. Richards*

Above: The review of incomers would not be complete without a glance at a few of the more unusual engines that called for only short periods. Two ex-Brecon and Merthyr 0-6-0STs Nos 7 and 8 as GW Nos 2'183 and 2184 were at Oswestry around 1926 to 1928. No 2184 had received 'the full treatment' with a Metro tank boiler and pannier tanks. Seen on 28 August 1926. *H. C. Casserley*

Below: Only a short wheel-base engine could work the army branch at Marchwiel Depot and *Gallo*, a Manning Wardle engine of 1888 was brought in. The Great Western had acquired her with the Fishguard and Rosslare Railways and Harbour Co in 1913. Between 1888 and 1906 she had spent some time in the Argentine. Seen at Swindon 16 August 1922. *Courtesy of L. T. George*

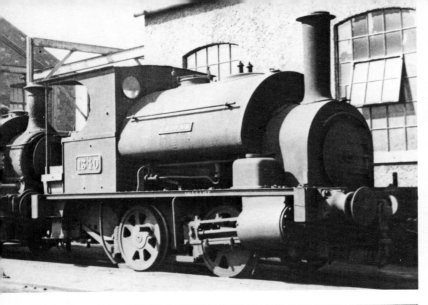

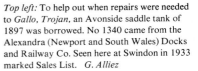

Top left: To help out when repairs were needed to *Gallo, Trojan,* an Avonside saddle tank of 1897 was borrowed. No 1340 came from the Alexandra (Newport and South Wales) Docks and Railway Co. Seen here at Swindon in 1933 marked Sales List. *G. Alliez*

Centre left: Another surprise resident was No 1677 once Brecon and Merthyr Railway No 20, an 0-6-2ST from the Vulcan Foundry in 1905. The Brecon and Merthyr was also a component of the Central Wales Division and B&M engines were repaired at Oswestry Works where safety valves and other standard minor fittings were put on. Photographed at Barmouth Junction 17 June 1925. *Ifor Higgon*

Bottom left: The 2-4-0 Metro tank No 1411 is on a Gobowen train, a reminder that Oswestry folk had been used to seeing small Great Western engines from way before the Cambrian had been formed. Seen on 28 August 1926. *H. C. Casserley*

Above: The Andrew Barclay 2-4-0T No 1308 off the Liskeard and Looe Railway had come to Oswestry almost immediately after Grouping to enable small Cambrian engines to be released for repair. She stayed there except for a brief spell on loan to the Culm Valley in 1929 until she was scrapped. C. B. Collett was very fond of her and on his instruction a special chimney pattern was kept as he felt that a standard one would mar her individualistic appearance. Seen here on a Tanat Valley goods c1936. *Anon*

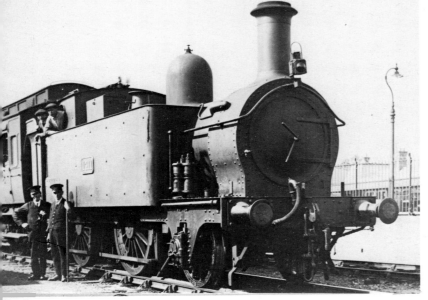

Right: Another of the little engines which helped to give Oswestry the title 'the home of the oddities', No 680 an 0-6-0ST was another representative of the Alexandra Docks. Their No 19 she was built by Pecketts in 1891 and when she needed repairs a sister No 679 was borrowed. Seen at Oswestry c1930.
R. E. Thomas

Below: The title 'The Oddest of Them All' should go to No 1376. She was built for the standard gauge Culm Valley Railway in the broad gauge works of the Bristol & Exeter Railway in 1874. In 1881 at Swindon she was rebuilt with an extra two feet into the wheelbase. She joined the Tanat Valley stud in 1927, and is seen here at Oswestry on 28 May 1932.
H. C. Casserley

Top: After the traffic side had ensured the continuity of services by releasing enough engines from outside, Swindon could get on with the refurbishing of the remaining Cambrian engines. Eleven of the 22 Queen class by Sharp Stewart & Co in the 1860s had lasted on including Nos 1 and 10 thus duplicating the numbers which were also carried by the second hand Great Western 2-4-0s bought from the Bute Docks Supply Co. Four of these small light 0-6-0s were retained at the request of the officers at Oswestry. In later Cambrian days they had been known as the Small Goods. No 14 as 898 at Oswestry 8 June 1925.
A. W. Croughton

Above: The usual first treatment was the provision of a new built-up smokebox with Great Western chimney, a four-way standard safety valve inside a brass bonnet and standard minor fittings. This tender has had a quick one-off treatment to increase the coal capacity. The other two of the class to be retained were No 45 as 900, No 48 as 908 and the

subject of this picture at Barmouth Junction on 16 June 1926 is No 51 now 910. *Ifor Higgon*

Above right: Fortunately none of the 10 Aston Goods (once known as the Large Goods) of the 1890s was lost in the scrappings of 1922-23. They were sound engines with no vices and the crews had a high regard for them. No 77 as 880 at Machynlleth in 1924. The character with the lamp has one foot on the jack which had been carried on all Cambrian engines after the Welshampton accident. *H. W. Burman*

Below right: The No 9 boiler mentioned on page 13 was evolved in both saturated and superheated forms. This is one of the Vulcan Foundry trio as revealed by the extra deep sand boxes on the leading splashers, No 78 as 881 after the 1924 rebuild. The other two were No 79 which became 882 and No 80 now 883. The seven of the type built by Neilson Reid & Co were re-numbered as follows, Nos 73 to 875, 74 to 876, 75 to 878, 76 to 879, 77 to 880, 87 to 884, and No 88 to 885. *W. H. Whitworth*

Top: The Jones Goods (which had been known as the Belpaire Goods) were handsome engines as built between 1903 and 1919 and although three were lost prematurely in 1922 the surviving 12 were destined for a long and useful working life. These were renumbered 15 to 844, 29 to 849, 31 to 855, 38 to 864, 42 to 873, 54 to 874, 89 to 887, 93 to 892, 99 to 893, 100 to 894, 101 to 895, and No 102 to 896. No 54 as 874 in unaltered condition at Towyn in 1922. *H. W. Burman*

Above: The same engine at Oswestry on 28 August 1926 after the full first stage treatment. She has a rebuilt smokebox with Great Western chimney, standard boiler top fittings; and the tender which has come off No 102 has been raised by welding a new strip of plating between the footplate and the old side to increase coal and water capacity and also has higher coal plates at the top. *H. C. Casserley*

Right: A rainy day in Wolverhampton, an old engine of the 1860s with the rods taken off and the paint peeling off, and a four-wheeled tender painted in a style which had been discontinued 13 years earlier. Cambrian No 53 once the proudly named *Gladstone* on page 33 in *Cambrian Railways Album* is on the way to the scrapheap. Four of the 10 Albion class had survived, and all were scrapped by the end of 1922. *W. H. Whitworth*

Below: Quite a number of engines ran for the first 12 months or so in Cambrian livery. Here Small Sharp Stewart No 50 has only the cast brass No 1110 to deny her otherwise Cambrian allegiance. There were six of this class built in pairs between 1878 and 1891. No 20 was scrapped unrenumbered. Of the others No 16 was renumbered 1115, No 17 went to 1116, No 21 to 1118 and No 60 to 1112. Seen at Llanbedr & Pensarn in 1923. *H. W. Burman*

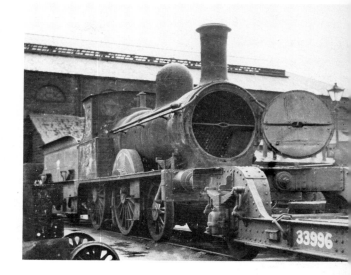

Above left: With the first 30 of C. B. Collett's new design of 4-6-0 the 'Castle' class in the offing there was no point in designing or fitting new boilers to the 4-4-0 types, some 'Dukes' and 'Bulldogs' would become available through the general downgrading; and more would follow as the 'Kings' and the 'Halls' came into being. Generally the Large Sharp Stewarts would be kept running with the minimum of expenditure until they failed and were condemned. No 61 as 1088 is here unaltered except for the safety valve. Seen at Oswestry on 8 June 1925.
A. W. Croughton

Left: No 19 as 1082 at Afon Wen in 1927 with the standard minimum treatment. Except for No 82 destroyed at Abermule, and Nos 65, 68, 70, 72, and 81 destroyed at Swindon, 16 out of the class of 22 engines ran on under the new management. The renumberings were Nos 11 to 1068, 19 to 1082, 32 to 1085, 47 to 1086, 61 to 1088, 62 to 1090, 63 to 1091,

64 to 1093, 66 to 1097, 67 to 1100, 69 to 1102, 71 to 1104, 83 to 1106 (and to 1110 in 1926 to clear the number for a new Dock tank), 84 to 1107, 85 to 1108 and 86 to 1109. *Anon*

Above: Of the four remaining crack express engines of 1904 (No 95 was lost at Abermule) No 94 was promoted to 1014, 96 to 1029, 97 to 1035 and 98 to 1043. The first two had been reboilered during 1920/21 and their old boilers were reconditioned in Swindon and fitted to No 98 as 1043 and to No 97 as 1035 respectively. Somehow none of the standard safety-valve bonnets would fit properly and the nearest that could be found showed the four outlets peeping over the top. No 97 as 1035 at Barmouth Junction is seen here running without one at all. The three classes of 4-4-0 are referred to as they are generally known in railway literature but the Cambrian designated them the Small Bogies, the Large Bogies and the Belpaire Passengers. *H. W. Burman*

Left: The three little Sharp Stewart tanks of 1866 were thoroughly and neatly Swindonised even to extending the coal bunkers over the buffers. No 57 seen here at Oswestry on 28 August 1926 became No 1192, No 58 became 1196 and No 59 became 1197. The other two 2-4-0Ts which had been converted from tender engines were scrapped at the outset. Even these three could not have consecutive numbers because in registering the absorbed engines the Great Western were just filling in gaps left in the lower numbers left by scrappings of old engines. The sitting tenants of the three numbers in the gap namely Nos 1193 to 1195 were at that time three elderly Armstrong Goods. *H. C. Casserley*

Above: The urgent plea from Oswestry saved three of the Nasmyth Wilson 0-4-4Ts of 1895/99. No 3 became 10, No 8 seen here at Aberystwyth on 4 August 1928 became 19, and No 9 became 20. Nos 5, 7 and 23 went in 1922. *Ifor Higgon*

Below: No 24 the Lambourn Valley 0-6-0 Hunslet tank *Eadweade* was one of the best small engines and retention was essential; and later she became No 819. There's probably a bit of practical joking going on here; the paintshop would have enjoyed putting GWR on such a diminutive engine. (See page 9.) Later they dwarfed her by just managing to jam the full Great Western transfers close together along the tanks. *Locomotive Publishing Co*

Above right: Both the Chapman & Furneaux 0-6-0Ts were needed and

emerged after overhaul in a jaunty Swindon style. No 26 seen here at Oswestry on 8 June 1925 became No 820 and No 35 became No 821. Thus with the three Lambourn Valley tanks the Great Western had sold to the Cambrian in 1904; once more they had had some of their own back. *A. W. Croughton*

Below right: Lastly the Grand Old Lady herself, the eldest of them all by one year. No 30 now 824 at Oswestry c1930. She came off the Mawddwy Railway and had been built by Manning Wardle's in 1865. This completes the tale of the engines taken over from the Cambrian except to mention that all six of the Metropolitan Railway 4-4-0Ts including the two tender conversions were condemned very quickly, only one ever had a Great Western number plate. (See page 10.) *R. E. Thomas*

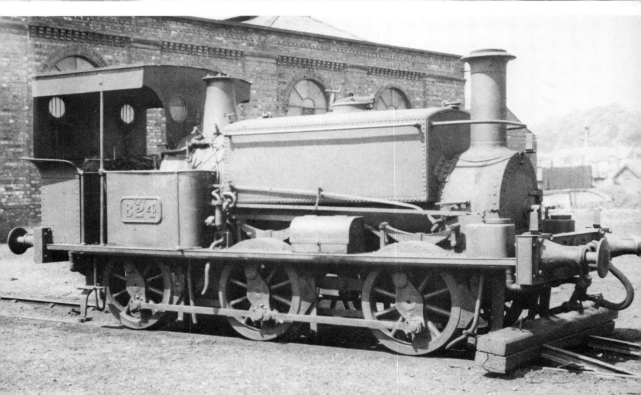

Above: Often engines of the absorbed companies lay around outside at Swindon Works for months awaiting work or decisions; and were duly photographed again and again. No 86 as 1109 was laid off in May 1923 was not formally withdrawn until January 1924. Seen here on 20 July 1923. *Anon*

Below: The biggest improvement the Great Western made to the Cambrian fireman's lot was to give him an additional firing hole at floor level. These were standard Swindon practice and were easily opened and closed by tripping the top-hung flap with a stroke of the shovel against the chain seen hanging down on the left. This meant a lot up Talerddig which could call for four 14lb shovelfuls a minute, and more with a heavy handed driver. And now for the bad news, the Great Western

shovels were bigger and heavier. Compare this photograph of No 83 as 1110 on Swindon dump in October 1933 with that on page 64 in *Cambrian Railways Album. S. H. P. Higgins*

Above right: The requirement of two new special engines for the 1ft 11$\frac{1}{2}$in Vale of Rheidol line was greeted with much enthusiasm at Swindon. Standardisation can become monotonous and a job in which all that could be taken from stock were cylinder castings borrowed from steam rail cars and a few minor fittings gave scope for real ingenuity. Nos 7 and 8 were built to replace No 3, *Rheidol* a tiny 2-4-0 Bagnall tank and to put the number of engines up to four. The other two original engines on which the new design had been based were Davies and Metcalfe 2-6-2Ts of 1902, No 1 formerly *Edward VII* became No 1212, and No 2 once *Prince of Wales* became No 1213. In 1924 that same healthy Repairs and Renewals Fund already mentioned quietly produced a complete set of parts for a third Swindon-style engine. Like Topsy she 'just growed' and the old Davies and Metcalfe outline bearing the number 1213 'just faded away'. *Great Western Railway*

Below right: Renewals were not needed straightaway for the 2ft 6in gauge Welshpool and Llanfair Railway. Great Western livery really suited both engines and carriages and they looked as smart as they had done when new in Cambrian bronze-green and white. Seen here in 1929 in Raven Square, Welshpool. *W. H. Whitworth*

Top: When the wholesale destruction of the more obsolete or worn-out examples of coaching stock commenced in 1922 someone had the foresight to instruct the photographer to record some of them. An alternative thought might have been 'If we don't collect a bit of evidence nobody would believe us'. Later, and perhaps to save 12″ × 10″ glass plates, they were recorded in whole rows. No 48 built at Oswestry in 1884 as a 1st/2nd composite had rot in the bases of the corner pillars and was scrapped in March 1923. *Great Western Railway*

Above: Brake Composite No 333 had just a six put in front of its number to become 6333. It lasted to run in the British Rail period so its journey to the works in a goods train did not betoken any major fault. Seen here at Barmouth Junction on 28 August 1926. *Ifor Higgon*

Bottom: The old Vale of Rheidol carriages also had the full livery treatment as did the four 'summer cars' built new at Swindon in 1923 to replace some converted toastrack four-wheeled vehicles which were not fancied at all. *C. Hollick*

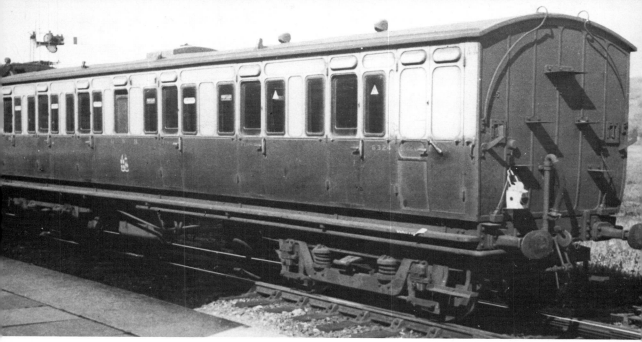

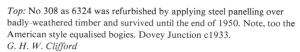

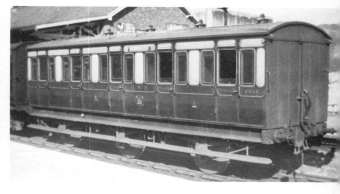

Top: No 308 as 6324 was refurbished by applying steel panelling over badly-weathered timber and survived until the end of 1950. Note, too the American style equalised bogies. Dovey Junction c1933.
G. H. W. Clifford

Above: No 268 a 1st/3rd Composite lasted as No 6282 until March 1948 and had been built in 1898. Photo taken c1933. *G. H. W. Clifford*

Above right: Of the 350 Cambrian passenger-rated vehicles nearly 200 were six-wheeled coaches. Some had to be used for a while but the general instruction was 'eliminate as soon as possible'. By the end of 1927 there were barely 50 left in passenger service along with two specials out of the 40-odd four-wheeled coaches and other passenger train includees. No 172 as 4066 with the paint faded a bit at Portmadoc c1930. *G. H. W. Clifford*

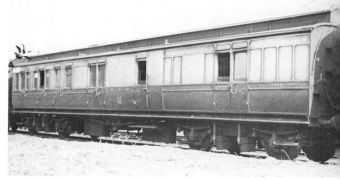

Right: Many of the handsome Dean clerestorey carriages were drafted in to replace the condemned Cambrians. No 2328 began life in 1900 as a three compartment/luggage locker/brake with diner alcoves, first class of course. In 1917. practical considerations overrode those of haute cuisine and the coach was stripped out, even to the removal of the first-class dog lockers, to make a roomier brake van, and was downgraded to third class. Seen at Penmaenpool c1934. *J. P. Richards*

Top: Of the 400 odd timber trucks only 70 or so were found to be fit for further use and all had gone by the end of 1931. No 1217 as 17031 with the twisted and shrunken deck planking first bolted down in 1919 lasted only until December 1928. *A. M. Gunn*

Left: The Cambrian had only 130 covered and ventilated vans and fewer than 60 were retained; only one survived into 1930. After all the Great Western had thousands of spare Minks as they were termed in the Great Western Telegraph Code Book. Strange-sounding names were given, sometimes with an allegorical slant towards use or appearance, and always to sound and look different from one another. No 57066 of 1891 at Barmouth c1923. *J. P. Richards*

Many many years ago in the days before station to station telephones the Cambrian had a tictac system for ordering empty goods stock for the following day. Arms swept from down to sides up to level with shoulders and stretched outwards followed by four handclaps meant four opens. Arms held upwards and sweeping down to level with shoulders as before followed by two handclaps meant two covered vans. These signals were given to the guard of the last goods train of the day if the train had not stopped and either the signaller had forgotten to write a message he could throw or he just could not write anyway. The guard had to duplicate the signs to show that he had understood. One evening as the last goods was drifting gently back to Portmadoc and the guard was standing on his balcony appreciatively spooning away at his soup he suddenly realised he was being signalled and true to his duty he signalled back. He was seen standing horrorstruck with his hands clenched tightly to the rail as he receded backwards away from the shattered steaming mess on the platform that had once been his lovely supper.

Centre left: Over 100 of the Cambrian's 200 or so cattle vans survived the initial stage and all those went in the 'root out all timber underframes' drive which was finally enforced during 1927 and 1928. Again the Great

Western had a good stock of Mexs from which to provide replacements. And the old Cambrian really did have a tictac sign for a cattle van too, fingers held up behind both ears. No 13854 had been built in 1901 and only just failed to survive into British Rail management. Seen at Barmouth c1923. *J. P. Richards*

Bottom left: Of the Cambrian's 47 horseboxes only 21 were actually found and identified and all but one of these were smashed up on sight, The replacements as evidenced by No 700 of 1893 were not as new, so there must have been something about the Cambrian design the inspectorate did not like. Seen at Penmaenpool, c1923. *J. P. Richards*

Above: Another strange-sounding name, this time for a furniture van truck. Horse-drawn furniture-removal vans could be sent by rail fully packed to be collected at the other end of the journey by a local team of horses. Serpent No 17477 had been built originally for the 7ft broad gauge in 1873 but was regauged only four years afterwards in 1877. Seen at Barmouth c1923. *J. P. Richards*

Top right: The Cambrian fetched most of its ballast for the coast from its quarry at Wern. Cambrian No 2384 still doing the same job as GWR No 31879. It had cost only £70/14/- (£70.70p) in 1902. Note the spats to keep the grit out of the axleboxes. Seen at Barmouth c1923. *J. P. Richards*

Centre right: By comparison No 2062 cost £78 put out to Ashbury's in 1897. At some time it has been made into a fixed side wagon, but the middle two hinge-bands are still there as stiffeners. As No 30993 it has Great Western OK axleboxes. Seen at Barmouth c1924. Generally the Cambrian's 1,700-odd timber-framed open wagons went to the knackers yard very quickly indeed; when marshalled at the head of the Great Western's longer trains they were apt to get torn apart. *J. P. Richards*

Right: Brake vans seemed to have had a better-than-average life expectancy. The Cambrian had 39 and only one was scrapped initially. Three were never found and 35 went on into Great Western service, No 9 as 8782 was not withdrawn until October 1957. Seen here at Sands Siding, Aberdovey c1927.
G. H. W. Clifford

Top: Typical of the extensive refurbishing given to some stations was this example in which the shorter of two trains crossing there was put inside the loop while the longer one was wrapped round it occupying the entire loop and points and parts of both ends of single main as well. A long loop was put in and a new down platform and shelter was built opposite the warehouse. The layout in the goods yard was improved and the appropriate re-signalling was erected to be controlled from a new standard-style Great Western box. Main line standards had taken over at Four Crosses. *C. C. Green*

Above left: A complete relaying and resignalling programme could produce a typical Great Western country junction anywhere. Seen here at Talyllyn North. *P. J. Garland*

Above right: Many of the old Cambrian signals were merely repainted in the new striped style. In Cambrian days they bore white or black discs painted on the centres of the arms. Down starter Llwyngwril 16 August 1935. *H. F. Wheeller*

Top right: In Cambrian days Talybont Halt had a narrow timber overbridge with a tiny square platform barely sheltering under it. Access was along a narrow gangway supported on the timber buffer-stop of the siding that once lay on the left. Besides a facelift for Talybont and Llanaber new halts were opened in practically every part of the area to foster the expected growth of holiday traffic. *C. C. Green*

GREAT WESTERN RAILWAY.
NOTICE
ALL PERSONS FOUND TRESPASSING
ON THIS RAILWAY WILL BE
PROSECUTED AS THE LAW DIRECTS.

RHYBUDD
OS CEIR UNRHYW BERSON YN
TRESPASU AR Y FFORDD HAIARN
HON FE'I COSBIR YN OL
CYFARWYDDYD Y CYFRAITH.
TRWY ORCHYMYN.

Above left: The new design of ribbed small-spectacled arms on tubular steel posts appeared in some installations, as with the East Down Home at Barmouth Junction photographed on 15 August 1935. It was remarked that whereas the old Cambrian posts had nearly flat tops the new ones had these long spikey ornaments. 'Oh yes, the Great Western men need the ornaments to show them which way up to plant the posts!' *H. F. Wheeller*

Above: More of a mixture, an old Cambrian box and gantry and one new Great Western gantry. Seen at Barmouth Junction 21 July 1934. *A. W. Croughton*

Left: It was left to the Great Western to provide any notices in Welsh, the Cambrian as a rule did not. Their cast-iron notices were headed CAMBRIAN RAILWAYS (see *Cambrian Railways Album* page 93) and these headings were economically subdued with black paint. Arthog 13 August 1935. *H. F. Wheeller*

Above left: An Aston Goods in unaltered condition shunting Tonfanau Quarry in 1922. *Courtesy of H. B. Evans*

Left: No 1 as 1329 piloting a 'Duke' on one of the new through trains from Aberystwyth to Paddington. The leading coach for Euston is still in London and North Western livery. Llanbrynmair in 1924 before the road overbridge was built. *A. Wilson-Jones*

Above: An 0-6-0 Jones Goods No 42 as 873 in unaltered condition, one of the last batch built by Beyer Peacock & Co. The train is a very nice mixture, a GW six-wheeled brake composite, two Cambrian six-wheeled lavatory semi-corridor composites, a Cambrian six-wheeled third and a Great Western bogie clerestory coach, like the leading brake it is still in all-lake or even possibly the earlier all-brown livery. Seen at Towyn in 1924. *H. W. Burman*

Below: A rare photograph, still in all-lake livery, steam rail car No 39 built at Swindon in 1905. Six were reported to have been sent to the coast in 1922 but some actually went to the Wrexham & Ellesmere branch, No 39 worked the Dolgelley to Barmouth local service and two more were at Machynlleth for Coast locals. Seen at Penmaenpool, c1924. *J. P. Richards*

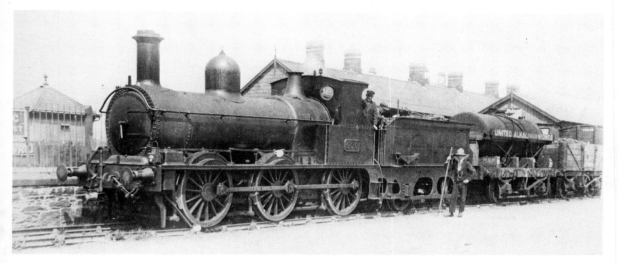

Left: In November 1922 the mountains showed the new masters what they could produce in the way of bad weather. The heaviest storms for years washed away tracks on the coast, and along the Dovey estuary and it was several days before services were restored over temporary track beds. An extensive programme of sea-walling and trackbed raising was put in hand immediately at Afon Wen (illustrated) and Llanaber. No longer would engine crews get soaked by waves bursting over the line during the winter storms. *Great Western Magazine.*

Below left: An 0-6-0 Aston Goods No 78 as 881 on the sea wall south of Harlech with her new No 9 superheated boiler and showing clearly the prominent rivet pattern round the smokebox which was to become such a feature on the rebuilt engines. Seen c1925. *H. W. Burman*

Above: An 0-6-0 Sharp Stewart, No 45 as 900 just arrived at Portmadoc on the down goods. The United Alkali Co's timber-framed tank wagon is worth a closer study. Seen on 11 June 1925. *A. W. Croughton*

Below: All six-wheelers, both Great Western and Cambrian, a 4-4-0 Large Sharp Stewart above the Harbour branch approaching Aberdovey, c1925. *G. H. W. Clifford*

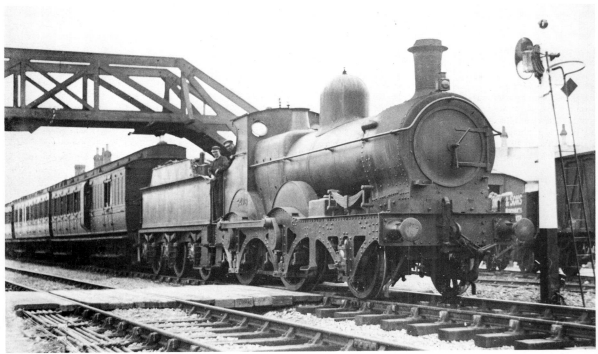

Above left: An 0-6-0 Aston Goods, No 87 as 884 shunting on the Sands siding at Aberdovey. Frequently after strong off-sea winds the track had to be dug out of the sand. Seen c1926. *G. H. W. Clifford*

Left: Barnum No 3208 on an up passenger at Towyn, c1926. The coaches are still in one of the all-dark liveries. *H. W. Burman*

Above: The 1922 floods had also covered the tracks at Aberystwyth and engines had been stranded at the shed with water lapping round the firegrates. The entire layout was rebuilt on a higher level and was formally opened in 1926. The design was lauded as English Renaissance and included a sprung dance floor; this was still the era of the 'Thé Dansant'. Alas by 1933 all this had passed and the restaurant would be let off as a telephone exchange. *Lewis The Mart-A. J. Lewis*

Right: The railwaymen's part in the General Strike of 1926 lasted only about a month and the Central Wales had managed to run a fairish emergency service. For one thing the railwaymen's wives were not in favour of it and nearly everyone in authority could drive, a situation not found at Crewe or Derby where the unions had opposed such a practice years before. One ex-Cambrian driver just back from the Argentine volunteered. Dubbed 'The Cowboy' it was averred that he was prepared to shoot his way through if need be. Less spectacular performances were expected of engineers and draughtsmen driving with bank clerks and insurance men working up good sets of blisters with the shovels. *Courtesy of R. B. Wilson*

THE STRIKE.

The thanks of the general community, as well as of the directors, officers, and shareholders of the Great Western Railway, are cordially extended to those members of the staff who proved loyal to the Company during the strike, and to the host of volunteers who readily and ably assisted the Railway to carry on. Grateful thanks are also tendered to the great number of others who placed themselves at the Company's call, but whose services were not actually required.

The loyal, constitutional spirit which actuated many employees to engage in any kind of work, and the enthusiasm of the volunteers, are in bright relief to the attempt by a small section of the community to coerce the Government of the Country.

It remains only to add that the affection of the public for the Great Western Railway could not have been more fully revealed and will live long in the traditions of the Company.

Above left: No 3264 *Trevithick* and a Barnum coming into the new station. Note the introduction of reinforced concrete signal posts; and the spotless condition of the platform. The leading flush steel-panelled coach would also be quite new. *A. J. Lewis*

Left: Once Great Western No 212, later the private property of A. R. Angus, after that Cambrian No 1 and now Great Western No 1329. She had a companion in her wanderings, No 213, Cambrian No 10 which by mistake got the lower final number 1328. Even the diagrams got mixed up and wrongly designated. Seen here on a neat little mixed train at Dinas Mawddwy, quite a change from piloting expresses. (See page 34.) *Courtesy of P. J. Garland*

Above: Much stress was laid on gaining first a Blue category route to the coast from Ruabon over Garneddwen, down to Bontnewydd where a crossing loop was put in and along the Dolgelley Branch to Barmouth Junction. Embankments were overhauled, old bridges like this one across the Gwynant were strengthened, and all was ready for the bigger and heavier engines. Jim Richards is measuring the clearance to see if there is still room for the mast of a boat. *Courtesy of J. P. Richards*

Right: In October 1927 the mountains struck again. Track was damaged all along the coast, a motor-boat was dropped across the track at Gogarth and much of the new work between Dolgelley and Barmouth was dislodged wholesale. *Great Western Magazine*

Mr. E. Shone.   Mr. T. Tudor.

Above left: A crash programme employing many extra hands from nearby farms was put in hand immediately. Whole sections were again raised even higher and the propped-up timber bridges were replaced in steel. Again the fight for a Blue route to the coast was on, and this time the engineers meant to win. *Courtesy of T. H. Jones*

Left: Another neat little train, 0-6-0 Sharp Stewart No 45 as 900 with the large tender off No 16, a GW six-wheeled locker and brake composite and an eight compartment clerestory bogie third. Seen here near Tonfanau on the 4.25pm Barmouth-Machynlleth local, c1927. This was her return working after taking the down goods from Machynlleth to Barmouth. *H. W. Burman*

Top: An unusual caller, Armstrong or Standard Goods No 877 of 1874 with the Engineer's Saloon from Shrewsbury at Barmouth Junction on 9 March 1927. *Ifor Higgon*

Above: Early in 1927 these two gentlemen, the Carriage Shop Foreman and the Wagon Shop Foreman retired 'under far more favourable circumstances than would have been the case under the Cambrian regime' as Mr E. Colclough announced when making the retirement presentations. Each received a clock suitably engraved and a pipe. All are to be found in the picture on page 9. The far more favourable circumstances of the day would by today's standards be somewhat meagre. *J. Maclardy, repeated in* Great Western Magazine

147

Above: A spectacular and rarely seen effect of steam; a gust of wind off the sea takes the smoke from a Barnum under its own train. As yet the heavier engines have not reached Barmouth. Barmouth Harbour Viaduct c1927. *H. W. Burman*

Top right: Unloading the SS *Onyx* at Aberdovey in 1927, using an open wagon as an intermediate unloading stage with a plank runway for the sack trolley to be wheeled into the waiting vans. The cargo was cement for work in the Elan Valley or on the Vyrnwy scheme; and was to be the last trade of any significance into the dying harbour. *G. H. W. Clifford*

Centre right: This shot from high level at Machynlleth conveys well the mixture of repainted and unrepainted companies' stock that was to be seen side by side for some time after the Grouping. As yet the Central Wales Division has no responsibility for the tiny Corris Railway. It was to the stationmaster at Machynlleth that a satisfied customer from the south wrote 'I thank you for the extreme courtesy and consideration of your staff, after I am through the Severn Tunnel I think I am on the Great Welsh Railway'. May 1927. *J. E. Kite*

Right: In India the coming of two trains face to face on a single track was termed a 'Cornfield Meet', like two persons meeting on the narrow path amid the head-high crop neither could go to one side without some damage. Abermule (*Cambrian Railways Album* page 99) was much discussed and its lessons much emphasised and a Royal Engineer officer told the author of seeing in the cab of an Indian engine a notice reading 'Look at your tablet remember Abermule', and repeated below in an Indian language script. Now look at the photograph on page 8', was this the doing of Chetma Bharsa? The 'Frontier Mail' of the Bombay Baroda and Central India Railway about to leave Bombay Walls, c1929. *Courtesy of Paul Towers*

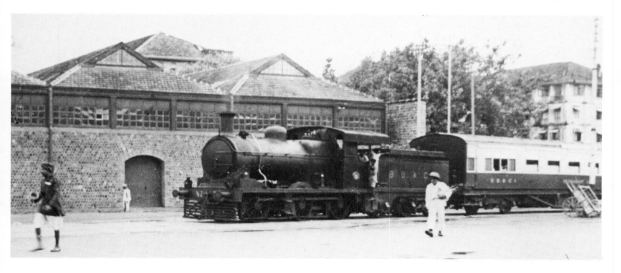

1928-1933
Slump and Revival

Railways had been allowed to increase their freight charges during 1928 but industrial depression was on the way and the increasing competition from road motors was working against them. The General Manager's report for January 1929 was not an encouraging one. Railwaymen's pay was cut with that of all services under government and local government control by 'The Geddes Axe' as the authorising act was nicknamed.

The Great Western Railway tried to beat the road competition by joining in and was very busy extending its country bus services and by inaugurating country lorry services; sometimes by buying out local cartage firms. In 1930 it acquired controlling interest in the Wrexham and District Transport Co Ltd and other local services in Wales. Controlling interests in Western National and Western Welsh followed in 1932.

Bulk petrol storage was a new business but the fresh revenue was not large enough to improve the overall situation by very much. Some railway

engineering work was authorised as part of Relief of Unemployment Schemes.

Welsh affairs were similarly in a decline, incomes and prosperity were well down. Between 1921 and 1931 over a quarter of a million people had emigrated and the population was barely 2.5 million. Of these 811,000 could speak Welsh and 98,000 still spoke Welsh only and the author recalls several happy overnight stays when touring by bicycle when communication was at first by signs, nods and smiles until the children or grandchildren came home from school; and then one chatted through them.

In 1933 a new source of income was tapped for the first time; old Cambrian land surplus to needs at Buttington was sold.

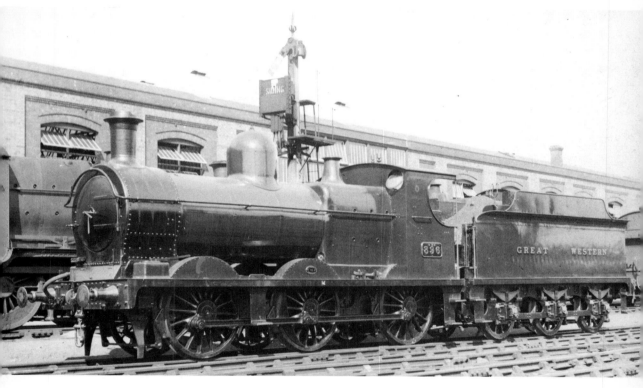

Above left: While No 45 had been entirely Swindonised in 1927 the other three little 0-6-0s remained as modified in 1924. No 14 as 898 at Machynlleth on 25 August 1931. *D. S. M. Barrie*

Left: A sight barely remembered, a warm muggy morning, a load of ice-cold water, and the whole of the tender water space is lined out in condensation. Aston Goods No 79 as 882 at Oswestry, c1929, with original boiler but added top-feed. *Anon*

Top: Before, 0-6-0 Jones Goods No 102 as 896 dumped after failing a boiler inspection at Oswestry on 28 May 1932. This is No 99's old boiler adapted with a Swindon superheater. *Anon*

Above: And after, outside Swindon Works on 11 September 1932, four months later, resplendent with her brand-new No 9 boiler. The tender now has extra-high coal plates. *A. W. Croughton*

Above: Mishaps like this to Jones Goods engines which had a bad hammer-blow defect in the driving axle as originally balanced set the mechanical engineers looking for a way of correcting the fault. Possibly at Llwyngwril. *Courtesy of Ifor Higgon*

Below: The Jones engines ran with the left-hand rods leading the right-hand rods by 90 degrees in match with the valve-events inside the frames. Trials on the static running bed at Swindon lead to the revision of events so that right-hand rods lead as in Swindon practice, to the boring away of the heavy weights on the driving axles, and to the addition of corrective weighting on all six wheels. The result was a sweet-running engine with 30% more power than a Dean Goods and

barely 10% below that of the new Collett Goods. No wonder they were to last for a very long time. No 15 as 844 at Oswestry on 12 October 1928, showing clearly the rebalancing of the wheels. Only two of the Aston Goods No 74 as 876 and No 88 as 885 were rebalanced; being pretty steady runners already little was gained thereby. *Ifor Higgon*

Bottom: A 4-4-0 Small Sharp Stewart, No 21 as 1118 at Kerry on 13 September 1929. With 0-6-0ST No 2075 she was working a long train of cattle vans for the annual sheep fair. It looks as if the extremely sharp curves have dislodged the second bogie splasher. She was condemned in 1930 and the class was then extinct. *Ifor Higgon*

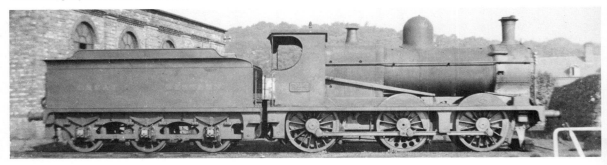

Above: No 63 as 1091 at Barmouth on 27 January 1930. With No 67 she went out of service only a few months later leaving No 83 as the last survivor of the Large Sharp Stewarts.   *Ifor Higgon*

Below: The last of the best Nos 94, 96 and 97 had all been withdrawn in 1928 but No 98 as 1043 stayed in service until January 1933. Still sound she was put on the sales list, as stencilled below the running plate, but no one wanted 4-4-0s in 1933, not even good ones and so she was cut up. *Anon*

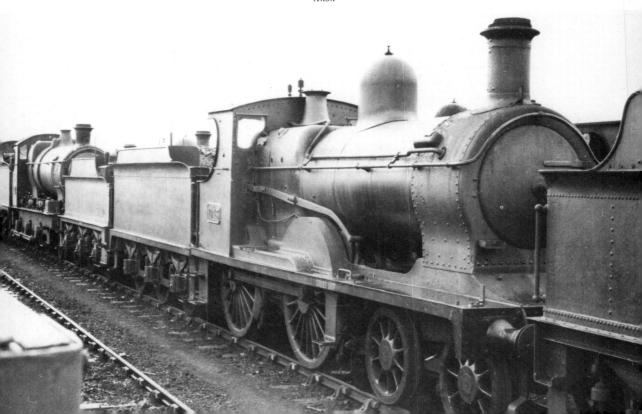

Above: The invaluable trio Nos 57, 58 and 59 kept going on the little branch lines along with old No 30 *Mawddwy,* the three Lambourn Valley tanks, No 680 the Peckett, No 1308 *Lady Margaret,* and No 1376 the Bristol and Exeter representative. No 58 as 1196 at Oswestry on 2 July 1931. *Ifor Higgon*

Below: Many more Dean engines worked over the Central Wales than those actually shedded there. Any one of them from Birkenhead, Chester, Croes Newydd, Shrewsbury, Tyseley or Wolverhampton were likely to be seen at Aberystwyth or Barmouth. No 2554 from Croes Newydd at Barmouth Junction on 21 February 1930 with the small 2,500 gallon tender. From 1930 when the first 0-6-0 Collett Goods were put into service these too worked in. *Ifor Higgon*

Above: In those days it was the drivers job to pack the regulator-rod gland through the backplate, and on the Dean domed engines the rod came out low down and close to the fire space. If the packing was done badly and the rod dropped to touch the casing, at best it meant a very hot handle and at worst a de-tempered rod. Barnum No 3219 in black livery at Barmouth Junction on 8 November 1932. *Ifor Higgon*

Below: A peaceful interlude at Plascrug, Aberstwyth in 1930. As the Cambrian 4-4-0s were scrapped more and more 'Dukes' which had been released by the construction of the modern standard classes were drafted in to take their place. *Cyril E. Mountford*

Above left: Blue category engines were allowed from Ruabon into Barmouth Junction by June 1927 but were not allowed across the bridge into Barmouth until 1929. No 3314 *Mersey,* the first 'Bulldog'to arrive at Barmouth Junction on 17 August 1928. *Ifor Higgon*

Left: One of the more extraordinary rebuilds resorted to at Swindon to maintain adequate motive power while wasting nothing. No 3559, once a broad gauge 0-4-2ST, later an 0-4-4T, and now a 4-4-0 raising its steam in a surplus-to-requirement boiler designed for a 36xx 2-4-2T. Seen here at Moat Lane on 20 May 1929, failed with a hot box off a Worcester to Aberystwyth excursion. *Ifor Higgon*

Top: 'Aberdares' first came into Barmouth Junction in 1928. No 2617 about to return to Ruabon on 31 May 1930. Having such small driving wheels the class needed more steam per mile travelled than their contemporaries and so when used on anything other than the very heavy coal trains for which they were designed they were extremely uneconomical in terms of their own coal and of fireman's effort. If the pressure was down when on a light train the steam reverser could slip back and this produced some very entertaining thumping noises accompanied by a sudden loss of power. *Ifor Higgon*

Above: Another fresh class appeared after the steam railcars had been withdrawn. No 1155 of the 517 class of 0-4-2T at Barmouth Junction while working the Dolgelley-Barmouth auto. The tiny boilers were a bit sensitive about their water levels, too low would obviously be unwise and too high readily caused priming. A good wheelspin could lift a lot of water over the surrounding landscape. The auto gear was jerky and could give very sharp regulator openings. Hence experienced crews ran with the gear disconnected and the fireman drove when running trailer first. Six dings on the cab bell could mean 'Inspector in sight, put the pin back quick'. *Ifor Higgon*

Left: Companies provided the vans for private maintenance contractors' employees. The Mawddwy Railway's ex-North London 1st/2nd class composite as Weighbridge Maintenance Van for Henry Pooley & Sons at Aberdovey c1930, a year before it was scrapped.
G. H. W. Clifford

Centre left: Great Western No 15 at Oswestry on the Tanat Valley train on 5 August 1935. There is a story about a lady who was doubtful about the withdrawal of the familiar old Cambrian carriages being re-assured that the new carriages would be good ones and complete in every way. 'Complete with fleas too I should not wonder' was the tart comment.
H. F. Wheeller

Bottom: At 38ft 6¾in this was quite the shortest bogie coach to run over Cambrian metals. No 2385 of 1894 had been built for use on the end of rakes of four-wheeled suburban commuter stock. Seen c1934 at Penmaenpool.
J. P. Richards

Right: Newer stock came in regularly on the long-distance trains in the summer services. No 3569 is a BarsII toplight design 57ft long, built in 1902. Seen at Barmouth c1934.
J. P. Richards

Below right: The two Observation Coaches Nos 176 and 178 made during the war from old Ashbury thirds were still very popular on the coast and as Nos 4070 and 4072 lasted until May 1936. Seen at Aberdovey, c1930.
G. H. W. Clifford

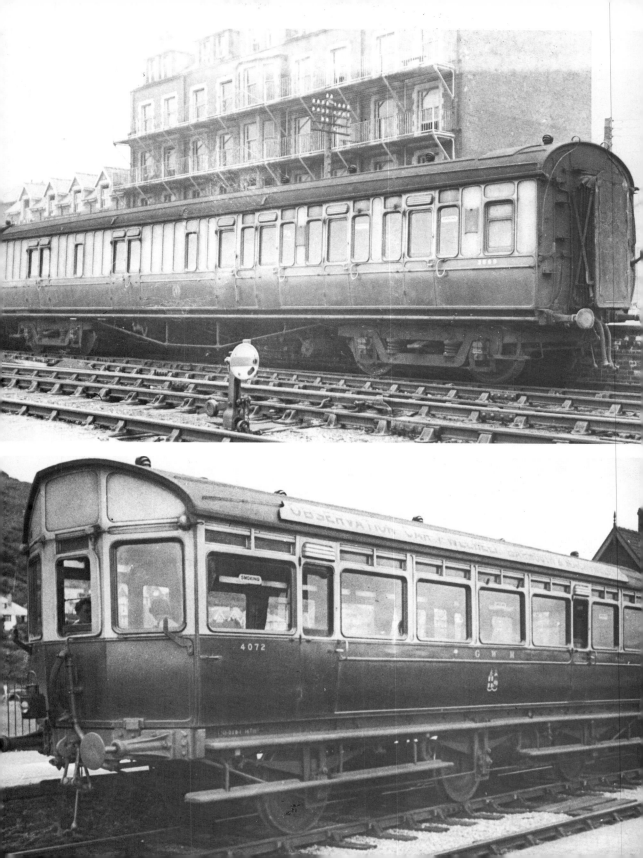

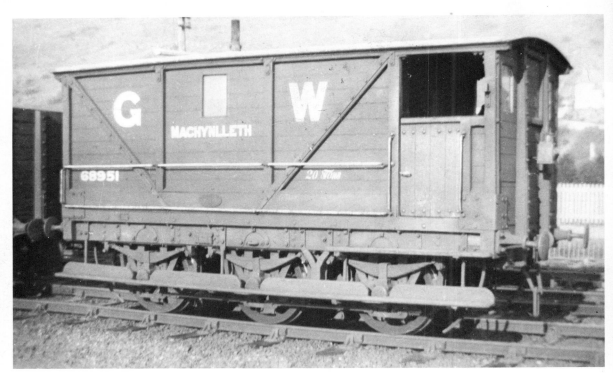

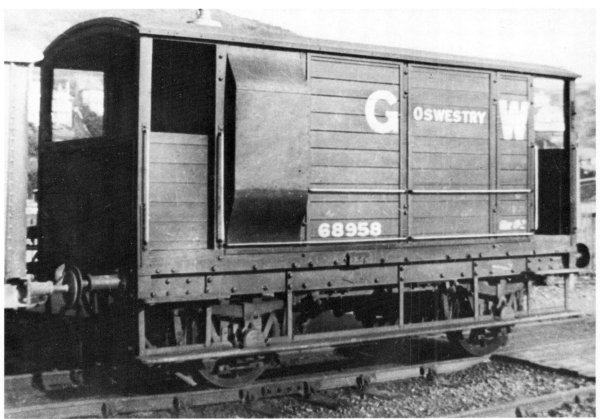

Above left: This goods oddity looked like a London & North Western brake van but was not. Built by Harrison & Camm in about 1899 as Port Talbot Railway's No 406. *G. H. W. Clifford*

Left: In 1918 financial straits had driven the Cambrian to buying some new goods guards vans built by the Metropolitan Carriage and Wagon Co through a Manchester finance company on hire purchase. Seen at Barmouth c1930. *G. H. W. Clifford*

Above: Doubts about Barmouth Bridge's capacity to take Blue category engines was resolved after a little remedial work by cautiously moving a pair of coupled pannier tanks across and watching the deflections of the structure yard by yard. Then followed a 39xx 'Hole in the Wall' tank coupled to a Mogul. Weakness was found only in Tunnel Viaduct across a little bay at the far end and this was filled in except for one opening used as a launching slipway; now the heavy engines could go right into Barmouth. By 1980 the timbers would be soft enough to be both harbour and larder for marine worms and the bridge would be restricted to DMU's only. *C. C. Green*

Below: The snag was that there was only a 45ft turntable at Barmouth and engines would have to make the double journey across the bridge to Barmouth Junction and back to get turned round on the triangle. No 3450 *Peacock* and a Mogul, c1933. *J. P. Richards*

GREAT WESTERN RAILWAY

The CAMBRIAN COAST
The Land of Romance

Left: A sky-borne charioteer, Harlech Castle towering above Beaumaris Castle and both guarding the same bay, all this and Owain Glyndwr with a Ronald Colman moustache, such were the commanding posters that lured thousands of holidaymakers to the bay of Cardigan in the 1920s.
Courtesy of R. B. Wilson

Below: Nor was publicity direct into the home neglected. The Handy Aids series of booklets were described as 'Dainty Little Volumes' and were free. This oné had 16 photographs, 24 pages of text and two maps; and a letter to Paddington enclosing an orange tuppeny stamp brought it tumbling through the letter box two days later. *C. C. Green Collection*

Bottom: The old Great Western terminus at Oswestry in 1928, with country buses and lorries parked under the canopy (around both sides). In the days of competition the Great Western would without warning retime a Gobowen train to leave just as the Cambrian train arrived. This caused the Cambrian to make a short-cut exit out of their station at the GW end; and some illicit smart running from

Great Western Railway

The Wye Valley
From Plynlimon
to Hereford
I.

Its Stately Castles, Matchless Ruins,
Old-World Towns and
Lovely Scenery

Llanymynech to arrive ahead of booked time.
Great Western Railway

Right: This interesting service from Devils
Bridge to the summit of Plynlimmon via the old
mine track from Eisteddfa Gurig and finishing
over the open mountainside was started by the
Kent brothers after World War I; but reading
the *Great Western Magazine* gives one the
impression that it was an inspiration at
Paddington that had brought it into being. Often
the trip was not completed and ended in a
derailment of a most unusual kind for a carriage
bearing the letters GWR.   *C. H. F. Kent*

Below: Here in 1929 a new sort of accident
occurred. A lady driver was badly hurt when the
train hit her motor car on the level crossing. Six
years later the train smashed into another car at
the same spot and killed Dr John Micah of
Machynlleth. Pedair Ffordd with No 59 as 1197
on the 5.25 from Oswestry.   *W. A. Camwell*

A Great Western entry which won the first prize in a recent Carnival at Oswestry.

(Driver T. ROBERTS).

Another Great Western "turn-out," which won the second prize in the same Carnival.

(Driver J. LUNT).

Above left: Hobbies and handicrafts were much encouraged and the principal exhibition of the best work was held at Paddington. It was usually opened by the General Manager now Sir Felix Pole and in 1929 the Oswestry apprentices' model of a Stephenson 4-4-0 made in 1904 was sent there to be a major exhibit in the very popular model railway section. It may now be seen in the National Trust Museum at Penrhyn Castle. *Great Western Magazine*

Left: The Great Western encouraged staff to take part in local affairs and permission to use company stock was readily given. Mr Roberts received the RSPCA's merit badge for the fine condition of the horses under his care. Oswestry Carnival 1929.
Border Counties Advertizer repeated in Great Western Magazine

Above: A 4-4-0 Large Sharp Stewart, No 63 as 1091 leaving Barmouth Junction. A goods train is waiting by South Box and No 1677 is showing steam in the South Loop. 23 August 1930. *Ifor Higgon*

Right: When the cab, top fittings, smokebox, nameplates and unbalanced cranks of No 3265 *Tre Pol and Pen* came back to Oswestry early in 1930 around a new boiler and on top of the frames of No 3365 *Charles Grey Mott* the combined engine made history. It was the brainchild of Mr K. J. Cooke who had the idea when he had the two engines side by side in B Shop at Swindon that the result would be interesting to build and should just come into Yellow category. She went back into service without comment until a few months later one of the Swindon staff enquired after her health and whereabouts. The reply was 'fine as far as we know and she's back at Oswestry'. Now the enquirer seems to have fotgotten that the new engine was a 'Duke' and no longer a 'Bulldog' and was most bothered that a Blue engine should have gone by mistake into a Yellow area, and he ordered her stopped and brought back light engine.

The Tyseley crew that was to have driven her from Aberystwyth to Birmingham that day was surprised to be ordered off her and given a Jones Goods to work the train to Shrewsbury. They left a bit late and pushed the Jones a bit hard. By Welshpool there was 'a bit of a pong', and the driver got down to have a sniff around and to feel the bearings. He looked up to his anxious fireman and confirmed 'two simmering, two frying and two cooked'. Actually he was leg-pulling; the Jones were made of good stuff and after taking things carefully up to Middleton Top the train was taken safely into Shrewsbury. Seen here at Oswestry c1930. *R. E. Thomas*

Above: A 2-4-0 Barnum No 3217 at the top of the steepest section of the Friog incline on 31 May 1930. *Ifor Higgon*

Below: A 4-4-0 'Duke' class No 3287 *Mercury,* receiving the token on the driver's side at Portmadoc, c1930. *J. P. Richards*

Above: A 2-4-0 Barnum No 3222 approaching Arthog on the 9.30am Barmouth to Ruabon on 23 August 1930. The leading coach, an ex-Cambrian 35ft six-wheeler is very much a survivor. By the end of this period there would be only five of them left in passenger service, and only one four-wheeler, the Royal Saloon. The Dean clerestory coach sagging in the middle looks rather tired too. *Ifor Higgon*

Below: A 4-4-0 No 3545 approaching Barmouth Junction on the 8.20am Machynlleth to Pwllheli on 23 August 1930, with some more modern stock for a change. *Ifor Higgon*

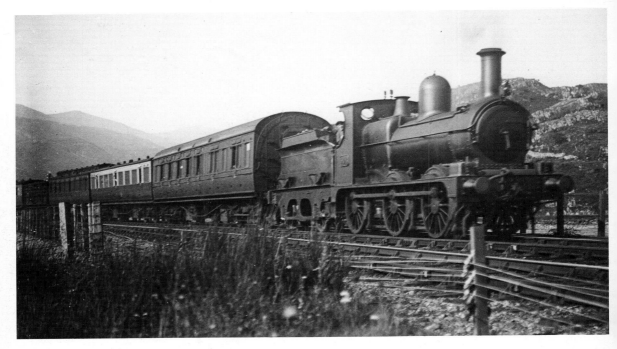

Above: A 0-6-0 Sharp Stewart, No 48 as 908 as fitted in July 1927 with a 2021 class pannier tank Belpaire boiler, a highly successful one-off experiment. Seen here on 1 September 1930 at Barmouth Junction on the 4.25am Barmouth to Machynlleth with possibly a unique mixture of stock. *Ifor Higgon*

Below: The replacement of the old Cambrian 'Kerry Donkey' by all Great Western components has left its charm undiminished. No 2075, a 2021 class saddle tank of 1900, a four-wheeled five compartment third of similar vintage and No 12022, an outside-framed goods brake of 1886 at Abermule on 7 June 1930. In 1895 No 12022 had been fitted with vacuum piping and brake-valve and sliding doors for use as a parcels brake van on the Helston branch. *Ifor Higgon*

Above right: A 4-4-0 Stephenson No 98 as 1043 showing a good turn of speed approaching Fairbourne on 17 July 1931. The mixture of eight and six-wheeled stock with its rising and falling roofline would made a very attractive model. *Ifor Higgon*

Below right: A 4-4-0 'Bulldog' No 3369 *David MacIver* leaving Arthog with the 9am Chester to Barmouth on 31 May 1932. In the 'Bulldogs' William Dean had attained a tractive effort nearly beyond the power of adhesion. The sandboxes on the later batches were cavernous and could take more than half an hour of fireman's time to refill especially if the engine was out on the end of the shed lines remote from the sand store; and with a heavy train the crew could need all of it and a couple of full buckets on the footplate for luck. *Ifor Higgon*

Above left: A 4-4-0 'Duke' class, No 3264 climbing with the 12.55pm from Aberystwyth near Commins Coch on 17 October 1932. Earlier on a fireman's idea of a nightmare was war reparations coal and *Trevithick*. 'Duke' fireboxes were deep down from the footplate, hard to de-clinker and little and often to each corner was the only reasonable stoking drill. But when you saw *Trevithick* you knew the fireman was having a worse time than usual, she, or he, was the worst steamer of the class.
Ifor Higgon

Left: The old Cambrian practice of having a ganger patrol on the Friog before the first morning train, had been discontinued as part of the general economies and on 4 March 1933 in the dawn light the 6.10am Mail from Machynlleth to Pwllheli struck a pile of debris fallen from the road above and history did repeat itself. Once again passenger carriages remained safely on the trackbed while the engine and tender plunged down to the beach, and once again the bodies of two railwaymen lay trapped in the wreckage. To Mr W. A. Spoonley, the slightest of build of all his companions, fell the sad task of working his way into the flattened cab to bring out the bodies of his friends before the sea came over.
Courtesy of Miss Evans Fernbank

Above: Another photographer in a white mackintosh takes a picture of the miraculously undamaged carriage. Then followed a strange event. At Oswestry works a scale model was set up, the engineers were not satisfied that the exhaust beat of the coasting engine could have, as was suggested, brought about the landslide; and two boys had seen an 18ft long crack in the road above, just after a 23ton lorry had gone by the evening before. Every time the scale measure of debris was slid down on to the moving model train it derailed but stayed above the model wall. Every time the model was run at a pre-laid model landslide it spun over the model wall; the landslide had to have taken place before the train came by. This must have been one of the first examples of a scale model being used to attempt to establish the cause of a railway accident.
Courtesy of Miss Evans Fernbank

Above: Unlike No 28 *Pegasus* of the 1883 accident No 54 as 874 was not recovered to run again; she had dropped from a much greater height. The heavy parts were cut up on the beach and all was hauled up in pieces as scrap metal. *Courtesy of Mrs C. D. Miller*

1934-1939
Holidays for All

The industrial recession had of itself partly receded and improved technology was putting up the rate of production. Trade union representation and general trends were moving towards the view that everyone was fairly entitled to an annual holiday with pay; and the Great Western had the engines and carriages to cope with the growing demand but it was only seasonal and would never restore railway prosperity which depended on the carriage of goods.

This was the era of Bank Holiday trains running in three or four portions calling into use stock that lay in sidings for most of the year. In the Central Wales Division the track doubling of earlier on was to show a great deal of benefit.

This demand for holiday travel buoyed up by the availability of transport brought a boom in seaside accommodation and many hard working Welsh families banded together to increase their income by making bedrooms and parlours vacant for visitors during the summer. Many too were the variations, a

hotel might reserve bedrooms in neighbouring houses and where mam managed all under one roof the children might be sleeping down the street at aunties' or at grannies'. It all added up to money for hard work and so the demand was satisfied.

Alongside all this the volume of goods traffic sent by rail was still falling and dividends, once $7\frac{1}{2}$%, were down to 3% by the beginning of this period. Worse was still to come and in 1938 the railways were making representation to the Ministry of Transport for 'Equal treatment with the road industry at the hands of Parliament' and for the removal of the 'Time-honoured shackles which fetter the Railways alone and well-nigh strangle their goods traffic.'

Population was still declining and many Welsh families found a little crock of gold by selling empty old cottages to visitors. Welsh speaking was still declining of its own volition but in 1939 the Urdd Welsh Language School was opened in Aberystwyth. It is not possible to judge what, if any, stimulus had been supplied by the Great Western ruling in 1937 that henceforth no working instructions were to be spoken in Welsh, but in history one can often discover the small happening that might have been another straw.

It appears to have been reported in one local newspaper only; just try imagining what the front

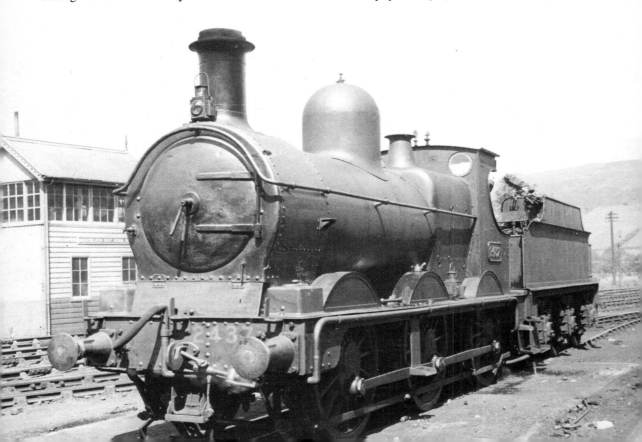

page headings would be if it had only just happened!

The previous sections will have been heartbreaking for those tidy minded modellers who like to see running trains of all matching stock; some improvement will be found in this one.

Below left: An 0-6-0 Deans Goods, No 2437 at Machynlleth on 12 August 1935. Over 100 of the 280 in the class were shedded in Central Wales at some time or another and most of those allocated in the Northern Division and many others worked in. The prominence of the Automatic Train Control shoe prompts the observation that in the Central Wales Division it was useless, they had no ATC and were almost the last to get it. *H. F. Wheeller*

Top right: An 0-6-0 Collett Goods No 2257 at Barmouth Junction on 25 June 1938 with an ROD tender. These were good engines once their first troubles with broken valves and crank axles had been sorted out, though the very sharp blast on full regulator could pull a lot of the fire up the chimney if the driver was pushing things too hard. Drivers on these taper boilered engines needed a fresh gadget, a piece of string. The lower quadrant regulators were comfortably light to move but could drop shut with the jolting. *Ifor Higgon*

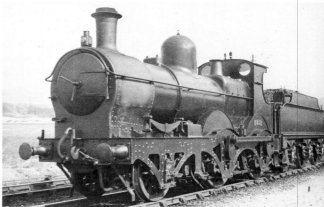

Right: A few Barnums only were left but all had gone by the end of 1937. No 3213 at Dovey Junction on 16 August 1935. *H. F. Wheeller*

Below: No 3284 *Isle of Jersey* at Aberystwyth on 16 August 1936. From now on the numbers of the 'Dukes' dwindled rapidly and by 1940 there were only 10 left plus *Tre Pol and Pen*. *W. A. Camwell*

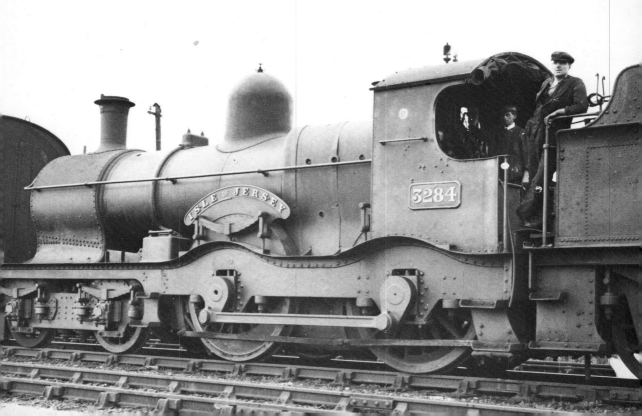

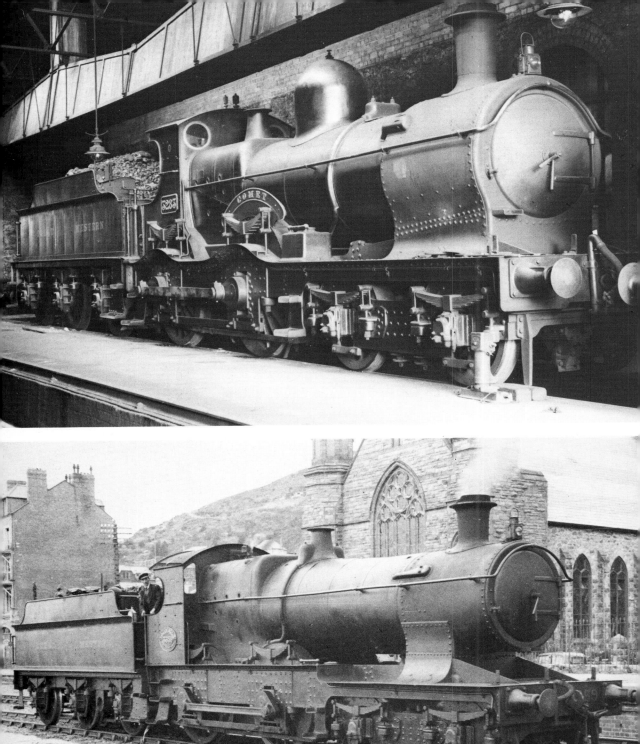
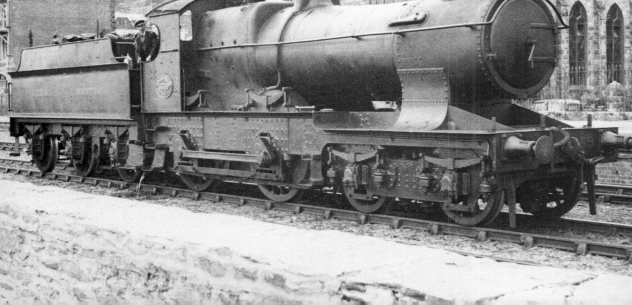

Above left: Poor old *Comet*, the victim of a perpetual joke. Someone found that if you yellow chalked IN in front of her name and AX after you had INCOME TAX. And she got 'done' again and again. The author saw the joke at Snow Hill, Birmingham; seen here at Machynlleth on 16 August 1936, unbesmirched. *W. A. Camwell*

Left: A 4-4-0 'Bulldog' No 3359 *Tregeagle* in Barmouth on 14 August 1935. These too were a dying class, Moguls were on the increase and by 1939 the first of the new 'Manors' would be feeling her way down to Barmouth Junction. *H. F. Wheeller*

Top: When the Assistant Running Superintendent from Swindon was making arrangements to visit Oswestry a return letter agreeing the date ended 'PS Bring up some more like 3265 in the bag'. This raised the question 'What was so special about No 3265?' (See page 61.) 'Duke' frames were failing and so the 'Earls' were borne of mixed parentage. 'Bulldog' frames and motion with 'Duke' boilers and fittings. No 3202 *Earl of Dudley* at Aberystwyth on 16 August 1936. *W. A. Camwell*

Above right: Most of the work down the Mid Wales line was done by the lighter engines, Aston and Dean Goods and 0-4-2Ts and a light pannier or two were all the line could bear. No 848 at Brecon on 6 September 1936. *W. A. Camwell*

Right: There were also a few light pannier tanks around Oswestry and Machynlleth, No 1924 at Machynlleth on 12 August 1935. *H. F. Wheeller*

Right: The four Sharp Stewart 0-6-0s had still kept going but No 51 as 910 finished in 1935 followed by No 48 as 908 in 1938. No 45 as 900 seen here at Swindon on 2 June 1935 after a very pleasing facelift, with No 14 as 898 became the last pair. *H. F. Wheeller*

Below: Only three of the Aston Goods would be left at the outbreak of war, No 79 as 882 on the Sales List on 3 March 1935. This was her second long spell at Swindon for nobody wanted to buy her and she had been there earlier between 1922 and 1925. *H. F. Wheeller*

Bottom: No 45 as 908 was transferred to Didcot from 1933 to 1937 and here in Didcot shed with a temporary supporting wheel while the front bearings were out for re-metalling she looks more like a 2-4-0. Seen on 21 April 1934. *H. F. Wheeller*

Bottom right: Aston Goods No 73 as 875 at Oswestry on 6 August 1935. Next year in October she was stopped at Machynlleth and condemned in the following December. *H. F. Wheeller*

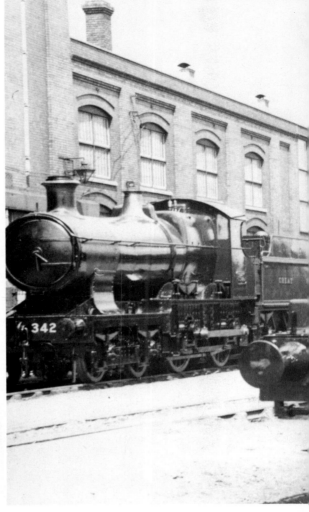

Top left: The Jones Goods were all in good shape and none was lost during this period. By now all had been rebalanced. No 38 as 864 at Barmouth Junction on 5 May 1938. To illustrate how versatile the No 9 boilers were, this one had formerly been taken off a Barry B class 0-6-2T. *Ifor Higgon*

Centre left: Jones Goods No 93 as 892 at Machynlleth on 12 August 1935 with a modern forward-drive lorry liberally plastered with the circular GWR totem devised in 1931 by Arthur Sawyer of the Publicity Department. It was ordered for general adoption in 1934 but took some time to spread round the rolling stock. *H. F. Wheeller*

Bottom left: The two Chapman & Furneaux tanks were successfully put on the sales list. No 35 as 821 went to Amalgamated Anthracite at Aberpergwm and was broken up in 1942. Here No 26 as 820 is at Mells Colliery on 18 April 1938. She was not taken out of service until 1945. *W. A. Camwell*

Above: No 236 now 6275 still looked very smart and effective on 16 August 1935 at Aberystwyth. Twenty three of this type of non-corridor and semi-corridor coach would be left by 1939. The larger roof water tank is a Great Western addition. *H. F. Wheeller*

Below: No 5956, a 57ft bow-end 3rd built in 1935 is typical of the flush steel panelled stock the Great Western had started building in the 1920s and which would replace most of the old coaches in the Central Wales Division by 1939. Seen here new in 1935 at Barmouth. *J. P. Richards*

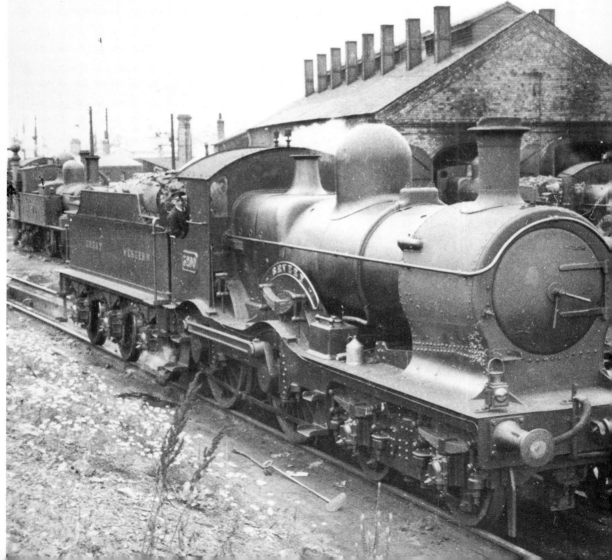

Above left: By now the railway-consigned goods of the Central Wales Division were carried almost entirely in Great Western stock. Known as the Small Mex these little cattle vans were not as popular with the farmers as the larger ones. It was sometimes possible to do a little cheating by moving the partition of a large van consigned as a small one; but the adjustments were locked by the top doors so that station staff could be alerted to jiggery-pokery by the early opening up of the vans. Now look back at the photograph on page 30. The use of quick-lime or bleach as cleaning and disinfecting materials which often caused tender or sore hooves had been prohibited. Seen at Oswestry c1935. *H. F. Wheeller*

Above: As it was with the carriages and wagons so it was with the engines, all were dying races. Only the tender of Jones Goods No 38 as 864 gives any clue that the shed scene is in a Cambrian area. Of the eight engines 'on shed' that morning five were Dean Goods and one was an 'Earl'. The two visible were Nos 2569 and 2449. Seen at Portmadoc on 16 August 1936. *W. A. Camwell*

Left: Another typical Great Western shed scene, there is just one alien Cambrian note, half an Aston 45ft carriage on the far right. 'Dukes' Nos 3290 *Severn* and 3265 *Tre Pol and Pen*. (She was always reckoned in 'Duke' stock and was never re-classified as an 'Earl'.) Seen at Aberystwyth on 16 August 1935. *H. F. Wheeller*

Above left: By accident however Oswestry shed only 10 days before had presented an entirely Cambrian appearance, provided one ignored the pattern of the top fittings. No 15 as 844, No 102 as 896 and No 59 as 1197. *H. F. Wheeller*

Left: Once the Dolgelley branch had been finally stabilised as a Blue route the term Ruabon branch was extended for all practical purposes to include the whole line between Ruabon and Barmouth Junction. Dean Goods No 2464 and 2-6-2T No 5174 taking an 11-coach Barmouth to Ruabon train out of Bontnewydd on 11 August 1934. The 31xx class tanks had been going to Barmouth since 1931. 3600 class 2-4-2 tanks also ran through to Barmouth on this type of duty. *Ifor Higgon*

Above: After this pattern of working had been established it followed that Cambrian engines would be seen outside their territory and into Northern Division country. Possibly No 31 as 855 on a Birkenhead to Oswestry train near Saltney c1934. *Anon*

Below: In January 1934 the Great Western announced its newest scheme for holidaymakers' accommodation at popular prices, the Camping Coaches; and the Central Wales Division came in for a goodly number of them. This was probably a group of staff posed at Dyffryn (the -on-Sea was added in the revision of duplicated names in 1924). The scheme was very popular for a while, especially with families with small boys. All that is missing from the picture is a notice reading 'The sea 1½ miles'. *Great Western Magazine*

Above left: 'Duke' No 3258 *The Lizard* near Commins Coch with the fourth portion of the 9.10am Birmingham to Aberystwyth on 4 August 1934. Possibly all the old excursion stock had been despatched in the first three trains and one of the Birmingham to Paddington sets has been brought up out of Tyseley, hence a matched set. Of all the 'Dukes' *The Lizard* will survive, cab, top fittings and cranks may be seen on the Bluebell Line as No 3217 *Earl of Berkeley*. *Ifor Higgon*

Left: Approaching Picnic Island bound for Penhelig and Aberdovey this Dean Goods with a pair of old clerestory coaches and a pair of bow ends makes a very attractive picture. *G. H. W. Clifford*

Top: When replacements were needed for the many lighter engines that were getting worn out C. B. Collett surprised everybody by building a fresh batch of 0-4-2Ts which combined all the best features of the old 517 class of 1868 as they had been successively modernised and rebuilt. The 58xx series built in 1933 were intended for work on the very light branch lines and as built had neither ATC nor auto gear. And so the Llanfyllin branch was the first to be properly modernised complete with flush-sided steel bow-end carriages. No 5816 seen at Llanymynech on 5 August 1935. *H. F. Wheeller*

Above: Reinforced concrete was then a very new engineering science as far as general practice went and the caption in the *Great Western Magazine* of the day referred to 'A Novel Engineering Achievement' and to 'Wonderful Modern Methods in Bridge Construction'. Court Pile Bridge over the Kerry branch near Kerry was replaced in 1935 when the original timber pile bridge was proving inadequate for road motors. *Courtesy of L. T. George*

Left: While it looked as if the Central Wales Division had been given the responsibility for running henhouses on wheels; in fact the Great Western's policy of taking over the local bus companies had brought in the charming little Corris Railway on 4 August 1930. Alas the first act was to close the line to passenger traffic as from 1 January 1931. Seen here below Esgairgeilliog 12 August 1935. *H. F. Wheeller*

Below: A 2-6-0 No 6399 approaching Dolgelley on a Barmouth to Chester train going via Ruabon on 12 August 1935. Up Garneddwen two of the smaller engines would have been needed and the Moguls were invaluable over this route. They were not officially permitted to run over the main line between Whitchurch and Aberystwyth nor over the bulk of the coast during the time covered within this book. *H. F. Wheeller*

Right: Since the destructive floods of 1927 the Arthog Bridge had been built anew in brick and steel resting on piles 55ft deep. It held firm against the flood of November 1938 from which the Stationmaster Mr W. T. Edwards escaped with his life by clinging to the levers of his ground frame up to his waist in a rushing torrent for two hours before the movement of the waters became still enough for him to move on to the roof of a hut. Hours later he was taken off by a boat from Barmouth. Auto tank No 4812 with Trailer No 164 on 13 August 1935. *H. F. Wheeller*

Below right: The Vale of Rheidol continued to run with its new engines and the old carriages which were getting worn out as shown by the sagging and bowed-down leading coach as compared with the renewed summer car behind. Note the boy in shorts selling refreshments. Seen on 15 August 1935. *H. F. Wheeller*

Above: 'Duke' No 3291 *Thames* leaving Aberystwyth with a train led by a pair of fine old durables, an Aston 45ft third and a Jones 54ft 6in corridor tea car (by now ex-tea car) on 16 August 1935. *H. F. Wheeller*

Below: For several years during the 1930s the amusing cartoons of A. S. Jenkins were an attractive feature in, it should be said, a very attractive and well-produced company magazine. He was quick to poke gentle fun at the visitors' problems when battling with the pronunciation of Welsh place-names. As is so often in Welsh humour there is a joke within a joke. Saxon is not really or usually used, well, let us say not as a compliment. *Great Western Magazine*

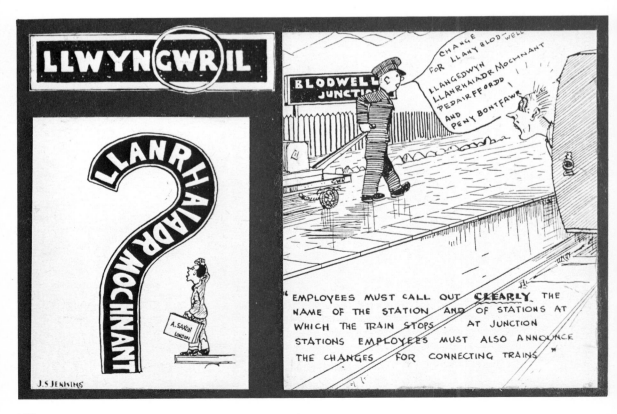

Above: Often Cambrian engines were to be seen in the works at Stafford Road, Wolverhampton, for repairs and repainting if Oswestry had too much on hand. No 99 as 893 beautifully 'done over' on 12 July 1935. In the old days No 99 was 'The famous 99', absolutely the best hauler of the class. Tom y Borth, always very jealous for his engine's reputation once was given an over-long train to take up Borth Bank and failed twice out of the station loop. He then overawed the signalman-porter into turning a blind eye while he backed about a mile towards Ynyslas and then tore flat out through the station and disappeared triumphantly out of sight at the top of the incline. Dare we say that in those days 'drivers were drivers'? *H. F. Wheeller*

Below: The slender Mid Wales bridges continued to give the engineers much cause for anxiety; and in 1926 the line south of Llanidloes had had to be downgraded to Uncoloured and the Large Sharp Stewarts and other 'Yellow' engines were no more to be seen along the valleys of the Dulas, of the Marteg and of the Wye. A programme of stabilisation by the casting-in of the triple pillars (see *Cambrian Railways Album* page 42) solidly into impressive mass-concrete arches was put in hand. Without this striking and imaginative solution to the problem the line would not have survived even as an Uncoloured route. 'M' bridge across the Wye below Marteg. *C. C. Green*

Above: By comparison with the careful preservation work on the Mid Wales bridges the Great Western were equally proficient at destruction. A really spectacular explosion near Overton-on-Dee early in 1936. To save maintenance costs an unwanted occupation bridge is demolished using '10lb of ammonal in 30 holes $1\frac{1}{2}$in + 12in detonated by a crank dynamo'. *Great Western Magazine*

Left: In the early 1930s much was written and spoken of 'economic maintenance' and it was considered that a motor trolley could well double the scope of a gang responsible for work on single line routes. The system was thereafter referred to as 'motor economic maintenance' and soon was in operation all round the Central Wales. Photographed at Kerry c1936. *Russell Tippetts*

Above right: The Llanfyllin branch may have been modernised but all the old charm of the Tanat Valley still obtained. The 2.15pm to Llangynog on 22 October 1938 with No 58 as 1196. She still had as her stable companion No 59 as 1197. *Ifor Higgon*

Right: Clerestories on two levels. 0-4-2T No 4874 on a Moat Lane to Brecon local train at Builth Road on 30 May 1936 only a month after being outshopped as a brand-new engine. Henceforth the Collett 'reproductions' would be a regular feature in the Central Wales landscape. *W. A. Camwell*

Above left: The author recalls walking round this competent display of modern signalling practice at the second British Empire Exhibition at Wembley in 1925. Years later he stood once more in the same signalbox looking at and handling the brass return tokens once issued to gold miners to allow them to pass over the adjoining bridge when journeying to and from their work. It had been put into store at Reading and was brought out again when Penmaenpool received a new 25 lever installation in 1936. Now a sign on the end reads Canolfan Hysbysrwydd Natur, Nature Information Centre.
From the booklet A Great Western Signal Box

Left: The Dethenydd range of hills, from which flows the Mochdre brook, whip up major storms and floods as efficiently as do the major and better-known mountains. When the track between Newtown and Moat Lane had been doubled the Mochdre Bridge very close to where the brook joins the Severn hard by Glendulais was left as the original single-track timber viaduct built by David Davies carrying the up line while a new single arch brick bridge was erected to bear the down line. In 1931 floods took out the brick bridge only and this was rebuilt.

In the house nearby, which constituted Scafell Halt, lived Mrs Haynes the stationmistress with her retired ganger husband and her daughter. In June 1936 befell a storm the like of which was beyond their experience

and, retired as he was Haynes made his way to the old danger spot accompanied by his daughter. After they had crossed the Mochdre a giant elm tree crashed into the swollen flood and careered downstream still nearby upright and wrenched both bridges to pieces, but leaving the tracks suspended across the gaps. The up train would come soon round a slight bend and on a fast section of the track, and the suspended rails could have deceived the crew into not observing that things were badly wrong. Miss Haynes battled through the wind and rain to Newtown to give the alarm while her father struggled round and got across the submerged road bridge only moments before it too was swept away; and telephoned Caersws to learn that his daughter had already reached Newtown and that the train from Aberystwyth was safely stopped.

The photograph was taken on 25 June, the morning after, and shows the fragments of both bridges and the sagging rails. Out of sight to the right the splintered remains of the trestle bridge lies athwart the Severn.
Courtesy of H. S Humphries

Above: Then the Great Western did what should have been done in 1915 and erected a longer single-span bridge. Look at the tiny trickle of the Mochdre in the summer and think how the Severn beyond could back up under flood conditions and impede the outflow of the tributary.
C. C. Green

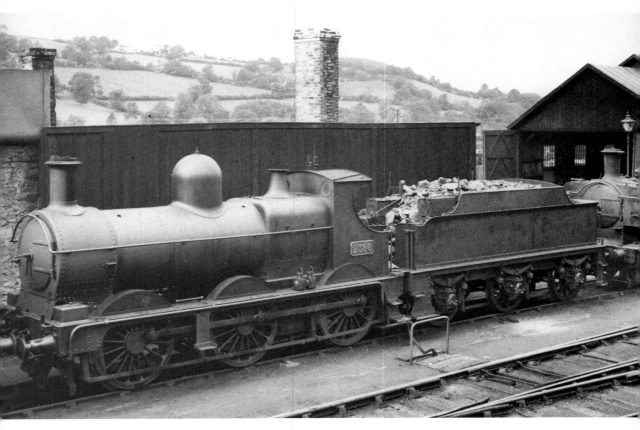

Above left: Reading the *Great Western Magazine* would not make one think they ever had any accidents. The first mention of the Friog came four years later in March 1937 when there was an article about the cliff-reinforcement work and the novel avalanche shelter where once 'a serious landslide' had occurred 'above the Great Western Railway'. A 2-6-2T No 5570 and Dean Goods No 2569 with the Portmadoc to Machynlleth Goods on 21 August 1936. *Ifor Higgon*

Far left: 'Duke' No 3257 once *King Arthur* alongside ex-London & North Western 4-6-2T No 6987 at Afon Wen in August 1936, just before the withdrawal of the 4-6-2Ts. *W. H. Whitworth*

Above: At one time little Brecon shed was the one the inspector could never fault, never a thing out of place. One of the men lived a little way up the line level with a 5mph speed limitation and his wife would keep an eye on the first-class compartments as the morning train crawled past. If she recognised the bowler hat she hung a red tablecloth on the line. Dean Goods No 2386 outside on 6 September 1936. *W. A. Camwell*

Left: By 1936 when Mr Spoonley retired as stationmaster of Builth Wells after 45 years on the Cambrian and on the Great Western the wearing of 'The Poached Egg' as the thickly padded badge was known had become as much a matter of pride as the wearing of the Prince of Wales Feathers badges of the Cambrian had been. He received 'a fountain pen and a wallet of currency notes' from his fellow railwaymen who also gave Mrs Spoonley a handbag and from the passengers, so much was he esteemed, there was a public presentation of a cheque. *Anon, repeated in Great Western Magazine*

Mr. E. Spoonley.

Left: The 4-4-0 'Earls' Nos 3210 and 3208 drawing the London and North Western Royal Train taking Their Majesties King George VI and Queen Elizabeth on the Dovey Junction to Afon Wen stage of their journey from Aberystwyth to Caernarvon during their Coronation Tour of the Realm. Heading North for Barmouth Viaduct on 15 July 1937. While at Aberystwyth Their Majesties formally opened the magnificent new National Libary of Wales (see *Cambrian Railways Album* page 84). *Ifor Higgon*

Below left: A number of industrial branches were being closed either through failure of trade or because road haulage outwards had become cheaper. Typical of the latter reason was Penstrowed Quarry Siding closed in May 1937. The quarry continued by using road haulage and is still working. *C. C. Green*

Below: After duty on the Royal Train No 3208, formerly *Earl Bathurst*, takes the Engineers Saloon back to Oswestry. Notice the immaculate finish still bearing the arms of London and Bristol, no 'shirtbutton' totem for them. Seen at Barmouth Junction on 15 July 1937. *Ifor Higgon*

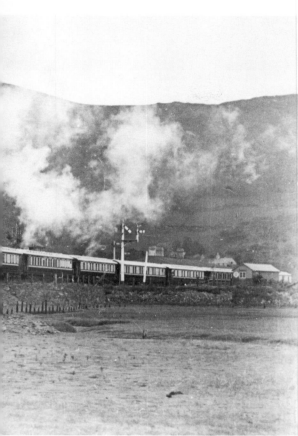

Above: One summer's day in 1937 Driver Jack Stubbs stopped for his fireman to climb down and then, lying down out of sight in the corner of his Dean Goods with just one hand on the regulator, he drove at a brisk speed with plenty of steam and smoke going up along Barmouth Viaduct. The last act of *The Ghost Train* was being filmed; and he was saved by trick mirror work, it was a model which plunged off the end of the opened bridge into the sea. *Courtesy of R. B. Wilson*

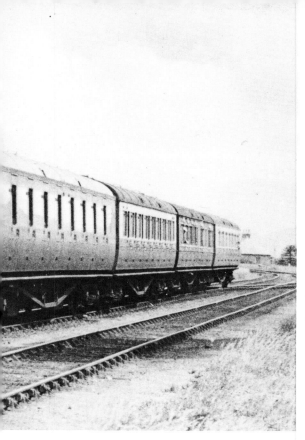

Left: The 4-4-0 No 3204 *Earl of Dartmouth* leaving Barmouth Junction with the 12.10pm Barmouth to Machynlleth on 26 August 1937. They seem to have been a bit tardy in removing the nameplate in Wales. When C. B. Collett started naming these Victorian-looking engines after the noble directors of the company he may have been indulging in one of his little touches of humour. In the event 'they were not amused' and the removal of all such nameplates for subsequent refixing to the next batch of new 'Castles' was ordered as from June 1937. Note: the author is not sure exactly when that modern sobriquet 'Dukedog' was coined but then they were the 'Earls' and to the Great Western they formed the 32xx class. *Ifor Higgon*

Below: Two walkers arriving here tired decided to take the train back to Aberdovey. After giving them the tickets, two tenpenny singles, 'That's tenpence the company are out of pocket!' said the guard, 'It costs half a crown in brake-shoes and coal to stop and start the train'. A 2-6-2T No 4549 and a Dean Goods passing Abertafol in August 1937. *Ifor Higgon*

Left: In September 1937 a strange assortment was unloaded at Llanbedr & Pensarn. There were ten horses, six goats, three mules, two tons of fodder, rifles, machine guns and a portable mountain battery. Zoltan Korda had come to make the open air sequences for yet another film, this one was *The Drum*. The picture here is a more normal one, on 9 August 1935, with Dean Goods No 2343 bringing another passenger train into the loop. *H. F. Wheeller*

Below left: Always eager to promote new business the company built several new warehouses with access by sidings specially built. This one was put in at the bottom of a long extension to the old siding on the up side at Montgomery in March 1938 for the Montgomeryshire Farmers' Association *C. C. Green*

Below: The opening of new halts had lost impetus, Carreghofa in April 1938 was followed only by Pickhill in the following month. (Tinkers Green opened in October 1939 was a special for the wartime use by Park Hall Army Camp.) The low bridge beyond the road bridge is the wrought-iron trough carrying the canal across the Llanfyllin Line. *C. C. Green*

Right: Jones Goods No 100 as 894 on the 9.40am Barmouth to Machynlleth rushing the bank from Fairbourne on to the Friog on 28 May 1938. *Ifor Higgon*

Below right: On the same day Dean Goods Nos 2536 and 2469 also making a good run on to the Friog with the Portmadoc to Machynlleth goods. *Ifor Higgon*

Above: A 2-6-0, No 6336, on the 2.35pm Barmouth to Chester on 28 May 1938 approaching Barmouth Junction. At last flush-sided steel-panelled stock is becoming the norm. *Ifor Higgon*

Below: Jones Goods No 31 as 855 banked by 'Duke' No 3290 *Severn* with two goods trains combined. Interesting that each goods train should also be conveying a departmental coach. Crossing Bells Bridge over the Machynlleth main road on 2 July 1938. *Ifor Higgon*

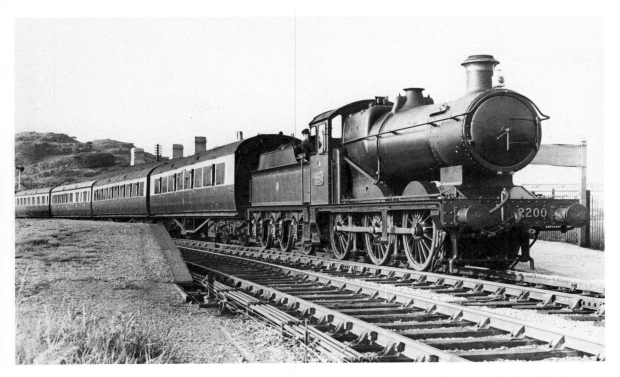

Above: A brand-new engine. The Collett Goods were not put out in exact numerical order of batches and No 2200 was the 50th to be built and they were known as the 2251 class. Seen at Barmouth Junction on a completely Collett style train on 23 July 1938. *Ifor Higgon*

Below: A 2-6-2T No 5517 and Jones Goods No 99 as 893 with a train of London Midland & Scottish stock clearly telling of 'foreign' origin. The returning Leicester to Aberystwyth Period Excursion on 6 August 1938 above Cemmes Road. *Ifor Higgon*

Above: 'Earl' No 3204 and Dean Goods No 2437 nearing the top of Talerddig Bank on the first Barmouth portion of the 'Cambrian Coast Express' on 6 August 1938. The first reference to this historic name occurred in the 1922 summer timetable as the 10.20am Paddington to Aberystwyth and Pwllheli. *Ifor Higgon*

Left: Often, if one of the senior divisional officers was keenly interested, a copy of a locally taken photograph might be sent to the editor of the *Great Western Magazine* to see if it was of sufficient interest to get inserted. Competitions were held for deft shunting performances and for the best kept length in each division and awards were made annually. In 1938 the prize went to the Talyllyn gang. *Anon, repeated in Great Western Magazine*

Right: Sharp Stewart No 14 as 898 pushing No 20's tender seemingly overlarge for her, leaving Llynclys on a goods to Blodwell Junction on 3 June 1939. *Ifor Higgon*

204

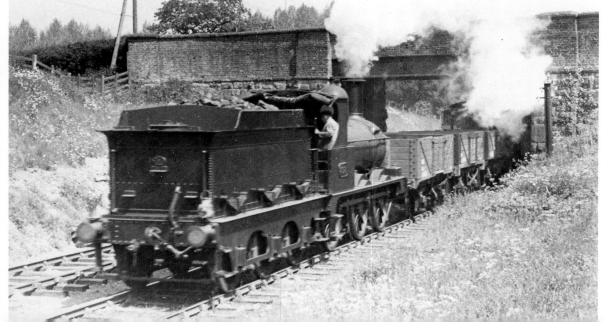

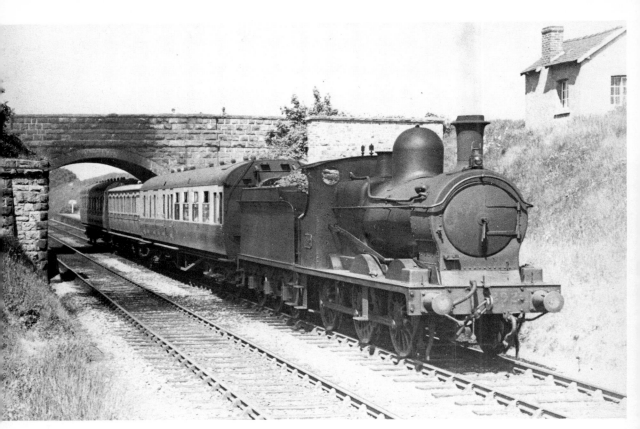

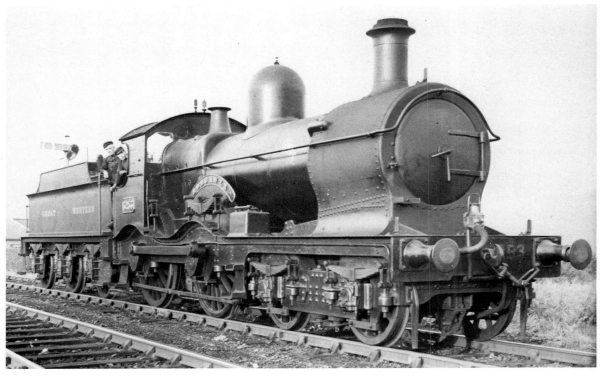

Above left: Jones Goods No 93 as 892 leaving Llynclys on the 2pm Whitchurch to Aberystwyth local on 3 June 1939. Central Wales could still produce a train of individualistic appearance. *Ifor Higgon*

Left: The Victorian Great Western engine. The second of the 'Dukes' No 3253 *Boscawen*; immaculate after 43 years of service. At Barmouth Junction on 9 September 1938. *Ifor Higgon*

Above: Old *Mawddwy*, No 30 as 824 ended her days in sedentary semi-retirement supplying steam to the engine which pumped water from Llyn Clys into the engine water tank at the junction. She finally stopped work in September 1940. Gone too by now were *Lady Margaret*, and all the other little one off tank engines from other parts; things around Oswestry would never ever be the same again. Seen on 4 June 1939. *Ifor Higgon*

1939-1945
Wartime Expediency

By 1939 even the Great Western with all its engineering efficiency and its brilliant Holiday Haunts series of publicity brochures was barely making its way and the shareholders had to be content with a dividend of a scanty half of one per cent. The motor lorry had nearly eliminated any chance of railway profitability and had the war not begun on 3 September 1939 nationalisation would have been inevitable if Britain was to keep intact any of the then strategically important railway systems. Now the author had to leave and observe, whenever time allowed, the railways of France, Algeria, Tunisia, Italy and Germany.

The Great Western was first off the mark in organising the first reduced wartime timetable to free passenger stock for troop movements; by 25 September the coast had four trains each way per day and there would be only a few extra trains on Saturdays.

The WD establishments at Park Hall and Marchwiel took on new leases of life and army camps along the coast made that section of the line as busy as it had been during World War I. The navy took over Butlin's holiday camp at Penychain as HMS *Glendower*. 'Blimey' said one raw matelot when detraining after a confusing and wearying journey round half the north of England and Wales 'Pennine Chain? We're still in ruddy Yorkshire!' After July 1940 he would not have known where he was; all station nameboards were removed so as to give no assistance to spies, fifth-columnists or parachute-borne invaders.

The Mid Wales line experienced the most noteworthy difference; instead of the Jellicoe specials thundering northwards on their long way to Scapa Flow carrying coal for the Navy there were the quieter trains loaded with limestone from Porthywaen coasting down the Wye Valley on their way to the blast furnaces of South Wales.

A total of 108 Dean Goods were taken from the Great Western for war service. All had Westinghouse braking added and some were converted into pannier-tender engines. Of the engines depicted in this book No 2437 was worn out at the end of her service and was scrapped by the War Department, as WD 191, No 2469 as WD 161 was converted to a pannier-tender and finally went to China under arrangements for UNRRA.

2-8-0s of the standard 2800 class as well as RODs had started to work to Barmouth Junction after 1937 and 1936 respectively as a result of a ruling to avoid the time being lost by using pairs of smaller engines; and were still arriving during the complicated rostering of the war years from as far afield as Banbury and Westbury.

Left: With so many Dean Goods away on war service the gaps had to be filled and at least eight ex-Midland Railway Johnson 2F 0-6-0s were drafted into the Oswestry-Moat Lane-Brecon area. Being unfamiliar engines they seemed reluctant to let them down Talerddig on the unwarranted assumption that they might not get them back up. At all events no positive memory of their having been seen at Machynlleth has ever been quoted to the author. No 3126 was at Moat Lane for a time. Besides these the occasional London & North Eastern J25 was known to have worked in, including No 1963. *R. J. Essery Collection*

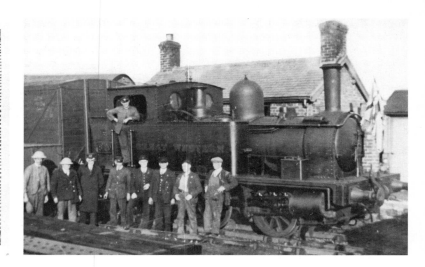

Above: Mottoes and slogans were pushed at everyone and while some of the politically inspired ones were pretty feeble this example which was to be seen on all the stations as well as at the sheds and in the messrooms did make sense. *Courtesy of R. B. Wilson*

Top right: While the connecting link between Nantmawr and Blodwell Junctions had been closed in 1925 the Van branch closure on 4 November 1940 was the Great Western's only severance of a limb of the old Cambrian system. A little last train ceremony was held with flags on the front of the Hunslet tank No 24 as 819. The ARP wardens are the stonemason and the blacksmith from the Bridge Department which was based in the old Van Railway Company's office at Caersws. The Hunslet ran until 1946, the last of the old importees to survive. *Courtesy of E. Morris*

Centre right: Swindon had treated the 2ft 6in gauge as well as it had the 1ft 11½in and finding the Beyer Peacock tanks as efficient as they had been built made new boilers for them in 1930. The new format of GW fittings really suited them. *The Countess* had to have a new nameplate cast reading just *Countess* to make way for the numberplate. Photography was not easy during the war and official permits were almost unobtainable. However one enthusiasts' trip was run and this photo was taken on 29 May 1941. *W. A. Camwell*

Bottom right: There was still a need for a lighter-than-standard engine to operate the Porthywaen sidings and in 1941 arrived No 1331 formerly Whitland & Cardigan Railway Co's No 3 an 0-6-0ST built by Fox Walker & Co in 1877. Seen here at Canton Shed in August 1937. *L. W. Perkins*

1945-1947
The Last Independence

The Great Western had always been prepared to continue in separate existence and had started to reintroduce some form of individual livery in 1942, a plain unlined black lettered GWR but the brief flash of wartime prosperity wherein profitability had been revived to the point of a dividend of around 4% being paid to the shareholders was over. The railways were back to run-down systems and to the peacetime reality of running costs in excess of receipts. Nationalisation had become a political issue regardless of rights or wrongs and this was a caretaker period when the railway people did the best they could with what they had to get things back to normal and hoped for better things to come.

Above: 4-4-0s Nos 3214 and 3222 approaching Cemmes Road with the 9.55am Aberystwyth to Paddington on 11 August 1945. A third engine No 5570 was banking. No 3214 has been recently reboilered and now has the more prominent top-feed casing which in the future will become a feature of the class. The carriage stock is once more a bit mixed and third in line is what we may now term an old clerestory.

Below: Standard practice on the non-standard gauge, but orders are orders and No 7 is a trifle dwarfed by the large initial letters. The coach evidences the entire replacement of the old carriage stock by new bodies and new steel underframes in 1938. Seen at Capel Bangor in 1946. *S. H. P. Higgins*

Above: The 10 'Dukes' with *Tre Pol and Pen* were still doing valuable service but were about to be renumbered into the 90xx series along with the 'Earls' to make the numbers clear for a new batch of the Collett 2251 class goods. No 3287 *Mercury* leaving Barmouth Junction with the 6.50pm Machynlleth to Pwllheli on 12 July 1946. The tender is still lettered Great Western with only the G and the W cleaned. The stock is still a mixture and in wartime all-brown livery. *Ifor Higgon*

Below: In July 1946 the engineers completed the fine long single-span bridge across the Severn at Buttington, their last major new work before Nationalisation. *C. C. Green*

Above: A reminder that the adjoining line at Llanymynech was put under WD control in 1941 and was the old Shropshire & Montgomeryshire. Great Eastern Railway Co's 0-6-0T No 388, later London & North Eastern's No 7388 as WD 70084; and Collett 0-4-2T No 4812 bringing in the 11.13am for Llanfyllin on 26 August 1946. *W. A. Camwell*

Below: The last two Sharp Stewarts No 14 as 898 and No 45 as 900 the latter having probably worked over more than a million miles had gone by the end of 1947 as well as the last three Aston Goods Nos 74 as 876, 87 as 884 and No 88 as 885 which had been condemned in 1939 and reprieved. So were left, grubby but unstoppable No 58 as 1196 and No 59 as 1197, both condemned in 1922, along with the 11 Jones Goods to represent the Dragon and the Rose under British Rail. Seen at Oswestry 10 May 1947. *W. A. Camwell*

Top right: The new 4-6-0 'Manor' class devised from the wheels and motion of a batch of Moguls first worked over the Central Wales down to Barmouth Junction just before the war and after 1942 had been allowed along the main line to Aberystwyth. No 7807 *Compton Manor* at Oswestry on 10 May 1947. *W. A. Camwell*

Centre right: Jones Goods No 31 as 855 with the tender off No 95 which had been destroyed at Abermule in 1922. Tender-swapping was a regular feature on all railways and the one crushed out of shape by the upreared distortion that had been No 82 actually belonged to No 92. This tender was miles away safely behind No 98. It had had four intermediate changes of allegiance before arriving behind No 31 in 1942. *Ifor Higgon*

Bottom right: There were still a few Dean Goods about. No 2572 leaving Barmouth Junction with the 6.15pm goods to Portmadoc on 25 August 1947. *Ifor Higgon*

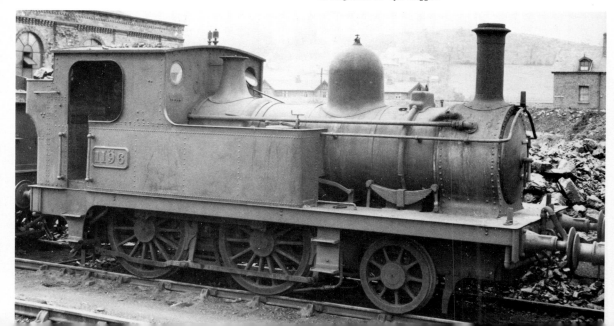

From GWR to BR

After 1922 the Great Western took over and for many years the Cambrian system provided the background for the most fascinating period of adaptation and conversion to be found anywhere in railway history. Cambrian engines were modified to such a degree that their own makers would scarcely have recognised them. Many attractive old Western engines were suitable for the work required of them in Wales and survived there, long past their allotted time.

Later all of these were supplanted by the standard types of engine evolved by British Railways. But the character of the line and its needs, although much reduced, remain to this day.

Right: A matter of balance. Old No 93, now Great Western No 892, shows clearly how, by boring four huge holes through the balance-weights on the central wheels and by adding weights in different places on all three pairs of wheels as dictated by tests on the Swindon test-rig, the 'Jones Goods' were made into reliable steady runners for many more years. *G. H. W. Clifford.*

Below: 'Swindon Magic' late on a November afternoon in 1932: No 3259 *Merlin* taking the Pwllheli train out of Barmouth Junction. *Merlin* was built in the 1890s as one of 'Mr Dean's specially designed hill-climbing engines' for use in Devon and Cornwall. *Ifor Higgon.*

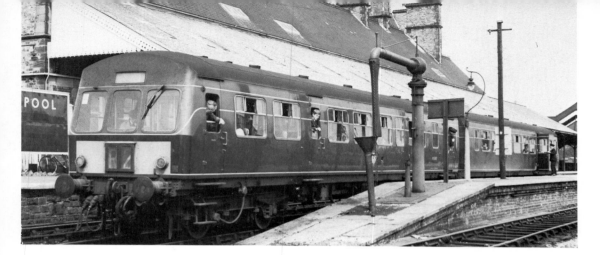

Above: The train had started to move when a passenger raced out of the booking office on the opposite platform and a shout from a porter halted it. Driver, passengers and guard all looked back while the porter shepherded him on board. So the old Cambrian courtesy towards its passengers goes on, reinforcing the Cambrian men's claim that in Wales it was they who took over the Great Western – and latterly – British Rail. *C. C. Green.*

Above left: Swindon through and through? No, just old Mid-Wales No 9 with a boiler and firebox made for a pannier tank, seen here on 27 August 1931 at Barmouth Junction on a goods to Machynlleth – as GWR No 908. The 0-4-2 tank is Great Western No 1155 off the Dolgelley branch. *Ifor Higgon.*

Left: British Railways Standard 2-6-2 tank No 82009 passing Barmouth South Junction on a Pwllheli to Machynlleth local, 15 June 1964. *C. C. Green.*

The Preservation Age

Preservation Groups operating in Wales have, fortunately for the Cambrian, been more in number and in vigour of action than they have been in many other areas. The Cambrian Railways Society has joined forces with the Welsh Railways Action Group, The Cambrian Coast Line Action Group, Transport 2000 (North Wales) and the North Wales Railway Circle in a Joint Working Party for the good of all the Welsh railway services.

Right: The Little Welsh Dragon. Truly the old Great Western has been proved to have been the first and the keenest of all the preservation societies. Their enthusiastic rebuild of all the stock in the 1920s has enabled the Vale of Rheidol line to survive in vigorous working order to this day. British Rail have sponsored The Vale of Rheidol Railway Supporters Association to enable the many people who wish the line well to have a direct interest in its continuing success. *C. C. Green.*

Below: The Welshpool & Llanfair Light Railway Preservation Co. Ltd was incorporated on 4 January 1960. While initially it used the two original engines, *The Earl* and *The Countess*, it very wisely looked elsewhere for more engines and rolling-stock and now runs the finest collection of different 2 ft 6 in or 760 cm gauge trains to be found anywhere. *The Earl* and *The Countess* are seen 'at rest' at Llanfair Caereinion in May 1975. *C. C. Green.*

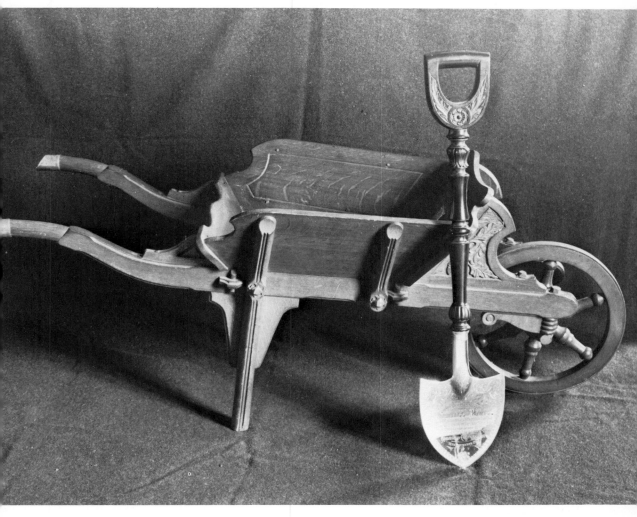

Above: The inaugural celebrations for cutting the first sods on the original little lines have left us with three ornate barrows and five elaborately engraved silver spades. This fine example was presented to The Countess Powis on 12 November 1899 by the Chairman and Board of the Tanat Valley Light Railway and may be seen at Powis Castle. The castle is open to visitors under the auspices of the Powis Trustees and the National Trust. *C. C. Green.*

Above left: Important arrival on Sunday, 12 January 1975. *Foxcote Manor,* which drew the last scheduled train from Oswestry, is housed for the Foxcote Manor Society in the old grain shed leased from British Rail by The Cambrian Railways Society Ltd. as part of their Oswestry operational headquarters. *The Border Counties Advertizer.*

Left: A coach with an interesting career – and a future. No 238 was built in the Metropolitan Carriage & Wagon Co's. works at Saltley in Birmingham in 1895 for £823. Described as a Diagram S, later Diagram 7 tricomposite, she served her passengers well until condemned as Great Western No 6277 on 7 January 1939. During the war she was Wireless Van 40576. Later she became Painter's Coach 80945 and went next to the Wolverhampton Bridge Department as a Mess and Sleeping Van. Now she belongs to Mr. Selwyn Higgins and is at Didcot for restoration. Before transit she was thoroughly vandalised and if anyone knows of the whereabouts of Cambrian axle -box covers, etc. . . . . Seen here at Herbert Road in 1969. *Selwyn Higgins.*

Above: No 4555 had arrived at Machynlleth shed by 1941 and she was bought by 'the two Patricks' Messrs Garland and Whitehouse in 1964 and one can now enjoy a journey behind here on the Dart Valley Railway. After a complete overhaul she was run in on ordinary service trains and is seen here leaving Snow Hill on a Knowle train. The two right arms above the cab side show that Pat Whitehouse is on the footplate with the driver. *C. C. Green*

Above right: The Cambrian Railways Society continues with much enthusiasm backed by hard work to rescue and recondi-

tion a very interesting collection of tank engines against the hoped for day when they will be empowered to run. Beyer Peacock 0-4-0ST of 1879 was at one time an 0-4-2 crane tank and is seen here moving No D7659 the last locomotive to be built by Beyer Peacock's in July 1966. *Anon*

Right: The Welshpool & Llanfair Preservation Society continues its policy of not wearing to extinction the two original engines by saving and bringing back beautiful engines which have been overseas. At Llanfair Caereinion in May 1979 is an engine from Sierra Leone. *C. C. Green*

Since these albums were compiled preservation has advanced considerably. At Oswestry the Cambrian Railways Society has been granted its Light Railway Order and is making short push-pull runs in steam on the last Sunday in the summer months with DMU runs in mid-month. The Vale of Rheidol has been much restored by its new owners, the Phyllis Rampton Narrow Gauge Trust and the Welshpool & Llanfair flourishes between its rebuilt terminals with its most attractive collection of 2ft 6in gauge engines and rolling

stock. Also of interest is the Vale of Llangollen Railway plc which now steams from Llangollen to Carrog along the Barmouth Road with engine types which appear in this book. It has plans for reaching Corwen. The Bala Lake Railway runs fascinating narrow gauge trains along that section of the 'Barmouth Road'.

The coach on page 220 is now restored and on view with much more of great interest in the Welsh Industrial & Maritime Museum at Cardiff.

Looking Back and Looking Ahead

We were not to know then that the 15 years before the war, when the dignified Victorian engines ran with their sleeker replacements, were the finest years for railway enthusiasts. The 15 years or so after the war were pretty good too and we did our best to record them with our, by modern standards, totally inadequate cameras.

How would the modern user of a 'Fix-it-all' camera cope if handed Mr Humphrey Burman's quarter plate magazine Klito camera with the plate manufacturer's instructions on how th guess the exposures? Alternatively there is the author's sixteen-on Zeiss Nettar with a top shutter speed of 1/175th of a second and the Burroughs Welcome date-and-time revolving weather card for working out the likely exposures. Then came the photo-electric exposure meters but, if the sun went in just as a black British Rail engine was appearing, one had to hastily push the lens open another half-stop.

Now, it appears, there are computer-driven scanners and integrators which, at the setting of very expensive buttons, are going to put all our mistakes right! But it still needs us, the old enthusiasts, to have been there at the right moment.

Ôl-nodiad

Felly y daw i ben hanes y Great Western yng nghanolbarth Cymru yn y blynddoedd hynny a adwaenir yn y dyfodol fel yr ail gynfod Georgiaidd yn ein hanes. Y mae'n astudiaeth sydd yr un mor ddiddorol â dim a aeth heibio, ac y mae'r gyfrol hon fel ei rhagfeisiau unedig Llundain a Bryste, mwy na Draig Cymru, Rhosyn Coch Caerhirfryn ac arwyddlun Tywysog Cymru, ar y trenau a'n cluda drwy'r wlad brydferth honno.

Postscript

So closes our story of the Great Western regime in Central Wales during what will be called in years to come the Second Georgian period in our history. It makes as interesting a study as anything that had gone before: and this book closes like its predecessor on a note of regret that the combined arms of London and Bristol, the red Rose of Lancaster and the Prince of Wales' Feathers in being seen no more on the trains which take us through that most beautiful countryside.